Ocean Birds
of the Nearshore Pacific

A Pomarine Jaegar (p. 114) flying overhead. (Mike Danzenbaker)

Ocean Birds

of the Nearshore Pacific

A Guide for the Sea-going Naturalist

Rich Stallcup

POINT REYES BIRD OBSERVATORY

Founded in 1965, Point Reyes Bird Observatory is a non-profit membership organization dedicated to conducting ecological research, interpreting research results to the public, and providing a scientific basis for conservation of birds and their habitats. Funding is provided by research grants, contracts, and individual contributions. PRBO provides credible, fact-based information and guidelines for policy issues and public and private environmental stewardship. Our studies of birds, marine mammals, and their habitats frequently involve issues of national and international significance, such as oil spill impacts, wetlands conservation, and wildlife/fisheries conflicts.

PRBO's publications are offered to the public to expand understanding and conservation of birds and the natural world. As the need to protect and enhance our environment for life in all its forms is increasingly recognized, an educated public is needed to make informed decisions. In our publications, we wish to share our knowledge of birds and other creatures — and our shared environments — to help inform and encourage people's awareness of ecological issues.

Printed in the United States.

Stallcup, Richard.
Ocean Birds of the Nearshore Pacific
A Guide for the Sea-going Naturalist
ISBN 09625918-1-5
ISBN 0-9625918-0-7 (pbk)

Designed and produced by Jon Goodchild/Triad.
Typesetting by TBD Typography

Jacket photographs:
Front: Pink-footed Shearwater, Rich Stallcup. Back: *Top right,* Tufted Puffin, Jeff Foote. *Middle left,* Sea Otter, Point Reyes Bird Observatory. *Middle right,* Leatherback Turtle, Ned Harris. *Bottom,* Fin Whale, Ron LeValley

PR BO

Point Reyes Bird Observatory
4990 Shoreline Highway
Stinson Beach
CA 94970

To the nearshore Pacific,
its magnificent wildlife,
its unpredictable moods,
and its awesome magic.

Acknowledgments

Very special thanks are due to:

My dad and mom, who yielded to my begging and let me continue getting on Farallon Island–bound boats (with Dad), regardless of my pathetic seasickness, from age eight onward.

Debra Shearwater, who during the 1980s allowed me easy access to the ocean arena.

Will Russell, who helped point me seaward on pelagic adventures all along both U.S. coasts, including Alaska, and southeast Australia.

Peter Pyle, who provided the most recent knowledge about birds of the deep blue sea.

Alan Baldridge, who knows *all* about Monterey Bay.

And my daughter, Willow, who is the light atop my boat.

Jon Dunn read and improved an early draft, Peter Pyle has generously looked over the manuscript several times, Kimball Garrett improved the proofs, and Guy McCaskie and Stephen F. Bailey provided some records from the files of *American Birds*.

Graphics were skillfully prepared by our friends Keith Hansen, Tim Manolis, and Ane Rovetta.

Because of their love for wilderness, Ewan and Helen Macdonald lent financial support.

Laurie Wayburn and the Board of Directors at Point Reyes Bird Observatory had the vision to see the project's end from the beginning.

Susan Claire Peaslee helped guide the course of this project from the first windy ripples through the monsoons and into snug harbor.

The following people have, in one way or another, influenced the production or content of this book:

David Ainley, Sara Allen, Caroline Arcoleo, Chris Arcoleo, Liga Auzins, Alan Baldridge, Dennis Beall, Rollo Beck, Louis Bevier, Laurence C. Binford, Alan Brady, Dawn Breese, Betty Burridge, Kurt Campbell, Harry R. Carter, Ted Chandik, Chris's Fishing Trips, Herb Clarke, Olga Clarke, Billy Clow, Howard L. Cogswell, Alan Craig, Harriet Crandall, Crazy Larry, Patrice Daley, Jim Danzenbaker, Abbie Dauterman, Dave DeSante, Ann Dewart, Jon Dunn, Art Earle, Dick Erickson, Jules Evens, Davis W. Finch, David Fisher, David Gaines, Sally Gaines, Roger Garcia, Kimball Garrett, Albert Ghiorso, Daniel Gibson, Connie Gottland, Leslie Grella, Judith Hand, Keith Hansen, Deyea Harper, Phil Henderson, Burr Heneman, Suann Hosie, Gene Hunn, Kenn Kaufman, Greg Kruse, Jerri Langham, Steve Laymon, Lisle Lee, Paul Lehman, David Lemon, Nick Lemon, Bill Lenarz, Gary Lester, Terry Lindsey, Cindy Lippincott, Lone Bear, Cliff Lyons, Guy McCaskie, LeAnn McConnell; Ann, Bill, Gege, and Tim Manolis; Al Molina, Michele Morris, Peter Metropulos, Joe Morlan, Adeene Nelligan, Jerry Oldenettle, Jane Orbuch, Gary Page, Ted Parker, Mike Parmeter, Susan Patla, Susan Claire Peaslee, Roger Tory Peterson, Robert L. Pitman, Point Sur Pirates, Rick Powers, Armando Quintero, C. J. Ralph, J. Van Remsen, Robert Rodrigues, Eleanor Roosevelt, Gary Rosenburg, Ane Rovetta, Richard Rowlett, Will Russell, Tom Sander, Barry Sauppe, Susan Scott, Maggie Seely, Debra Shearwater, Marianne Shepard, Dave Shuford, David Sibley, Arnold Small, Larry Spear, Dick Spight, Jean Stallcup, Lee Stallcup, Lynn Stenzel, Mary Anne Stewart, Art Taber, Scott and Linda Terrill, Stu Tingley, Tinker, Elizabeth Tuomi, Richard Turnello, Bill Tweit, Phillip Unitt, Dick Viet, Terry Wahl, Laurie Walton, Arthur Wang, Peter Warshall, Laurie Wayburn, Janet Wessel, Jack Whetstone, Jon Winter , and Diane Ziola.

The following people generously provided original color slides that we converted to black-and-white prints:

Stephen F. Bailey, Alan Baldridge, Dawn Breese, Bruce Broadbooks, Herb Clarke, Paul Crawford, Dorothy Crumb, Mike Danzenbaker, Jon Dunn, Jules Evens, Gary Friedrichsen, Ed Greaves, Ed Harper, Ned Harris, Alan Hopkins, Thomas Jefferson, Joseph R. Jehl, Jr., Leroy Jensen, Tom Johnson, Bill Keener, Peter LaTourette, David Leal, Ron LeValley, John Luther, Alan McBride, Tim Manolis, Roger Marlowe, Greg Meyer, Ann Miller, Gerry Mugele, Rod Norden, Jane Orbuch, Point Reyes Bird Observatory, Peter Pyle, Mark Rauzon, Don Roberson, Tom Schwan, Debra Shearwater, Bruce Sorrie, Larry Spear, Barbara Spencer, Craig Strong, Jack Swenson, Izzie Szczepaniak, Ian Tait, Dan Taylor, Bernie Tershy, Alan K. Thomas, Mark Webber, Richard Webster, Mike Wihler, David Wimpfheimer, Jon Winter, and Tim Zurowski.

Contents

Preface

Although this book will be useful for identification of oceanic vertebrates, it is not meant solely as a field guide. Instead, through use of photographs, it is hoped to be more a tribute to the animals themselves — their beauty and grace, their rugged delicacy, and their share in making Earth wonderfully diverse. It is also hoped that people who see this book will be taken by the wildness and freedom of these creatures and, when chances to defend the health and integrity of ocean habitats arise, will act strongly in accord.

The ocean waters of the Pacific adjacent to the coast of California provide some of the finest and most easily accessible seabird and marine mammal watching in the world. At any time of year, short and usually pleasant boat trips may record huge numbers and a great variety of pelagic birds, as well as several species of marine mammals — often including a couple of kinds of the Earth's great whales. For inshore areas between the beach and the continental shelf, the submarine topography, eternal collisions of several major currents, and generally cool, nutrient-rich waters contribute to this abundance. The year-round mild weather (a description that might be argued by veterans of some of the more bouncy rides) and the wide choice of harbors and boats make the logistics of "getting there" relatively easy.

In the past 20 years our knowledge about the surface animals of these inshore waters, their seasonal distribution, and their relative abundance has grown — so quickly that it easily surpasses all previous understanding. This renaissance is due in the largest part to regular, systematic searches by birders on pelagic trips conducted by Audubon Society chapters and nature tour companies and by more scientific surveys by such organizations as Point Reyes Bird Observatory, the National Oceanic and Atmospheric Administration, the National Marine Fisheries Service, and museums and universities. Enthusiasm has been greatly fired by increasing numbers of people interested in the nature of the world, its birds and animal life in general, and, especially in recent years, the whales.

Beyond inshore waters into the relatively stagnant "deep blue sea," much less is known, and biologists are just beginning to pioneer the region. For birders, that area remains a rather inaccessible frontier. Here, we creak open the porthole with new knowledge and some teases and guesses at the future.

For each bird species in this book, discussions include descriptions of plumage and behavior, notes on how to separate the species from similar ones, and in general, the timing and distribution of the species in the area covered. Because of the ebb and flow of food sources that birds follow, predicting abundance or locality on any one day or even one month is futile. Trying to structure a chart (such as a bar graph) does not work. Though many dates of occurrence for rare birds are included, others are missing, and this book is not intended to be a compendium of records.

Because my knowledge of marine mammals is less thorough (and more derived from published materials and discussions with friends), the species accounts in this section are shorter. Photos of cetaceans in their natural habitats show only bits and pieces of the animals (backs, dorsal fins, blows, or flukes). These photographs show how you will see the animals from boats, though, and thus are much more instructive than drawings or paintings of whole animals.

Quite unlike the bird and mammal fauna *on* the North American continent, which is well known, that of the oceans remains alien and enigmatic. To the human mind, the wanderings and life histories of pelagic animals remain mysterious.

There are no experts or masters, just students. It is as it should be.

RICH STALLCUP

Foreword

The sport of birding has grown almost explosively in recent years because of the proliferation of modern field guides. Pelagic bird watching is a relatively recent spinoff of this popular pursuit.

More often than not, watchers at the window, "chickadee or nuthatch type of bird watchers," become hooked on serious birding and sooner or later venture away from the back yard. They may even drive to some coastal hotspot or desert oasis to look for unusual migrants. Some may join the other binocular carrying folks at any of a hundred hawk lookouts across the land. Or, they may go out to sea. Pelagic trips are the "in" thing these days, the only remaining frontier in avian fieldwork.

My own memorable first pelagic bird trip in California waters took place more than 50 years ago when I was a young man gathering material for my *Field Guide to Western Birds*. My friend Guy Emerson, who was then treasurer of the National Audubon Society, had taken a boatload of Californians a few miles off Monterey and shown them their own albatrosses. When he returned to New York, I listened with rapt interest to his story, and he promised that he would take me out to see the albatrosses if I would bring along my cameras. *Life* magazine, hearing of our plans, wired Peter Stackpole, one of their staff photographers, to run up from Los Angeles to join us. So in the early morning of 23 May 1940, five of us gathered in a diner near the waterfront in Monterey, eager to start out. Around us at the counters sat young all-night revelers, boisterous and bleary-eyed, eating their scrambled eggs before going home.

At dawn we boarded our boat, the *Pleasure II* with Captain Arcoleo at the helm. We had brought along three large cans of oil, 20 pounds of chopped suet, and two buckets of squid. We started the slick while still in the harbor so that we would have a following of gulls, which in turn might attract the albatrosses when we were out far enough.

We had hardly reached the harbor mouth when we ran into great milling rafts of Sooty Shearwaters, spreading like a dark carpet over acres of water while feeding on some sort of swimming crustacean that swarmed on the surface. Many of the shearwaters, resting gull-like, were so stuffed they could hardly get underway as the prow of our boat bore down upon them. Some flipped aside, others dived in panic. We estimated between 15,000 and 20,000 Sooties, an unbelievable contrast to the scattered few that we see off the Atlantic side of our continent. They had come a long way from their breeding grounds in the Southern Hemisphere.

Black-and-white Pigeon Guillemots buzzed by, their bright orange feet straddling the air. A score of Black Brant hugged a barnacle-encrusted rock. Parties of cormorants passed continuously. A flock of 200 Pacific Loons, all in breeding plumage, flew in a northerly direction and close to the water in a long straggling skein. A flock of 20 Sabine's Gulls flew out of the fog at close range. They were in exquisite breeding plumage, northbound from the coast of Peru to their summer home in the Arctic. Storm-petrels of two species flitted by, and while we studied them the bird of Coleridge finally appeared:

At length did cross, an albatross,
through the fog it came.

We poured the oil and threw out handfuls of suet. The albatross banked, its long wings cutting the air like sabers, came about, lit on the water a hundred yards aft, and gobbled up our offering.

It ate the food it ne'er had eat,
and round and round it flew.

Soon there was a second albatross; like the first, it seemed to appear from nowhere. Another came, and another, until we could count 15 around the boat. The captain said that in 25 years of fishing in these waters, he had never before seen more than one or two at a time.

By putting the motor at its slowest speed we could drift down on little parties of 4 or 5 birds until we were only several feet away. We even tossed squid that they caught in their horny bills, just as you might throw bread to the tame ducks in a city park.

On that warm May morning in 1940, as we doled out our offering, all seemed well with the world. As our goodies gave out, the "gooneys" scaled off, one by one, to be lost in the long gentle swell of the Pacific. We did not dream that the drolleries of these confiding birds would soon win the affection of legions of American men stationed at Midway and other nesting islands to the west. We did not know that their watery world would soon become a theatre of war.

Today boat tours specifically planned for birders are scheduled regularly from several key points along the Pacific coast, from San Diego to Vancouver and even Alaska. Pelagic trips are becoming increasingly popular with hardcore birders as well as whale watchers, and because of this we are finding that some seabirds we once regarded as accidental may prove to be of regular occurrence if we go out far enough and often enough.

This new book by Rich Stallcup of the Point Reyes Bird Observatory takes us a step further in developing our skills at identifying seabirds. He discusses not only the obvious field marks but also the more subtle details, and especially the general impression and shape of the bird as it glides over the waves or faces the wind on some distant rock or sandbar.

Rich Stallcup is not only a star birder, the most well informed expert on California seabirds, he is also an excellent teacher who goes further than just the naming of species — he knows their behavior, population dynamics, and interactions with the environment. No one is more skilled at the game than Rich Stallcup, and in these pages he shares some of his secrets and insights about these ocean wanderers.

ROGER TORY PETERSON

The Fascination of Seabirds

The open ocean poses one of the harshest, most unyielding environments on the face of our globe, an environment that covers almost two-thirds of planet Earth. It is a vast, featureless place that can be calm and tranquil one day, turbulent and windswept the next. Hell could cause no greater despair than being cast adrift miles from landfall in a full-blooded gale. No desert could be more of a navigational challenge than a featureless ocean. Yet it is possible to go to the rails of a ship hundreds, sometimes thousands, of miles from the nearest point of land, look seaward, and see birds. These are no ordinary birds. They are the great adventurers of the avian world. They are *seabirds*.

Since time immemorial, seabirds have captured the imagination of poets, writers, and mariners — so much so that you can find them woven into the folklore and legend of mankind the world over. They are the little-known nomads of an oceanic realm. From the seemingly frail and vulnerable Wilson's Storm-Petrel, reputedly one of the world's most abundant birds, to the waddling tuxedoed penguin, from the ungainly pelican to the peerless albatross of legends, seabirds have evolved a mystery and aura of their own.

Land, where they all return to breed, is a place of unaccustomed danger for the majority of seabirds. Their real home is a world far removed from our own. Their chosen habitat is the open ocean, and there they feed, rest, and travel, often covering vast distances.

Many find their way over a featureless seascape with no visual clues save the heavens, by which they must orientate and navigate. Some, like the Arctic Tern, embark on vast journeys of many thousands of miles, traveling from one hemisphere to the other, and in so doing banish winter from their lives. How do they do it?

One can only marvel at the countless thousands of Wilson's Storm-Petrel chicks that, unaided and unguided, successfully migrate high into the Northern Hemisphere and then find their own way back to the last wilderness, Antarctica. There are no adults to show them the way or teach them how to feed, sleep, and survive over the ocean. How do they do it?

Think also of the most basic of seabird adaptations: the ability to exist for weeks, months, even years at a time over a saline ocean without the need to drink fresh water. For most life forms, including ourselves, even a few days without fresh water would spell disaster. Seabirds are quite used to ingesting prodigious quantities of salt water without ill effect. How do they do it? The average terrestrial bird will search for food within 400 yards of its nest and youngsters. An albatross will fly in excess of 1,500 miles to gather food for its youngster. How do they do it? They do it all because they are seabirds, the avian world's most specialized flying machines and its last great colonists and adventurers.

In a world of rapidly expanding knowledge there remain many more seabird questions than answers. This is no surprise. As land-based mammals, we have tended both as professional and amateur ornithologists and birders to concentrate on landbirds, as these are the more easily observed and studied. But in recent years there has been an explosion of interest in the oceans of the world, and in the life beneath and above the waves.

Pelagic seabirding voyages mean more than just adding new species to one's life list, or to a country's list of recorded birds. They have shed valuable new light on hitherto little understood parts of seabirds' yearly routine as they wander the world's oceans. Above all else a pelagic birding trip is immense fun, exciting, and surely the high spot of any birding calendar. Nowhere is the global pelagic push more apparent than where it all began — California.

It is for those of you lucky enough to live along North America's West Coast shores, and for those of you who visit this area, that this excellent guide has been written. The author needs no introduction. Rich Stallcup has an international standing, his reputation already established.

Certainly you will experience hardships in your quest for seabirds, but the harder the journey, the sweeter the success. Amid the howls of the wind and fierce hiss of waves breaking over the bows, there will be the ecstatic shouts of "Wilson's," "skua," or "Buller's!" It is those moments that linger forever and that will separate you from mere birders.

Welcome to the world of seabirding. I wish you everything from Short-tailed Albatrosses to Mottled Petrels as you help push outward the periphery of our seabird knowledge.

PETER HARRISON, Lands End, England

Introduction

In the following pages we will talk about the wonderfully abundant and diverse bird life that occurs (or may soon occur) in the nearshore Pacific off the coast of California. For our purposes in this book, the nearshore Pacific is here defined as a rough rectangle of ocean bordered on one side by the California coastline and on the other by a replica line 200 miles to the west. The state border with Oregon to the north and the international boundary with Mexico to the south complete the definition. These dimensions are set by the American Ornithologists' Union (and followed by the California Bird Records Committee) for the purpose of defining an avifaunal region.

Within this nearshore zone (out to 200 miles), we will call the waters above the continental shelf *inshore* and those beyond the shelf break *offshore*. The birds themselves easily cross from one definition to another.

We are concentrating the geographical scope of this book on the California Pacific not for provincial reasons, but because that is the area that we know most thoroughly. Although status and timing of ocean birds are marginally different south, at least to the tip of Baja California, and north along the coast as far as northern Alaska, this book will be widely useful in these areas as well.

Bird Groups Included

It is the birds that spend the *largest part of each year* on the open ocean that are the subject of this book. Truly pelagic (oceanic) by nature, many of these creatures prefer deep-water habitats well offshore, but many range into inshore waters. Those treated here include the tubenoses or Procellariiformes (albatrosses, fulmars, gadfly petrels, shearwaters, and storm-petrels); some Pelecaniformes (tropicbirds, boobies, and frigatebirds); two of the phalaropes; jaegers and skuas; some gulls and terns; and the alcids.

A few birds that have occurred nearby but which are not yet documented as recorded in the California Pacific are also included. They are White-capped Albatross (specimen offshore Washington State), Solander's Petrel (seen beyond the 200-mile limit), Juan Fernandez Petrel (occurs off southern Baja), Town-send's Shearwater (regular off Southern Baja), and Red-legged Kittiwake (specimens from Oregon and Nevada!).

A number of bird species that frequent nearshore, and occasionally offshore, waters are not considered truly oceanic birds. Three species of loons, six of grebes, three of cormorants, Brown Pelican, some gulls, some terns, Brant, and some ducks are usually an interesting part of pelagic trips — the part leaving and returning to the harbors — from August through April. They are not included here.

Life in the California Current

The waters just off the west coast of North America, from Alaska to Southern California, are most unusual in the global oceanic scheme of things: they are moving, mixing, and amazingly rich with life. A hundred miles wide and flowing vigorously from north to south, pushed along by the northwest winds, the California Current is one of the world's rare *eastern boundary currents*. These currents belong to great rotating systems, called "gyres," that circulate water completely around the ocean basins. Eastern boundary currents abut the west coast of continents, and, though totalling only one-thousandth of the world's ocean surface, together they account for over *one-third* of the world's fish harvest. (The other three eastern boundary currents flow next to South America, South Africa, and the Canary Island region.)

The reason why eastern-boundary-current regions are so productive is that nutrients are blended into them due to active coastal upwelling. Water in motion in the Northern Hemisphere is offset to the right (a result of the Earth's spin), so the California Current moves surface water offshore. At the edge of the continent, this surface displacement acts like a pump. It forces water up from near the sea floor, where all the nitrates and phosphates from ocean life have settled. When plumes of cold, fertile water reach the surface (especially in spring, when the northwest gales really *drive* the current), they fertilize meadows of microscopic plant life under the sun's rays. The entire food web thrives on this bounty, from pink swarms of krill (euphausid shrimp) to apex predators such as seabirds.

By contrast, the ocean is something of a desert out beyond the California Current. Like the vast majority of Earth's ocean

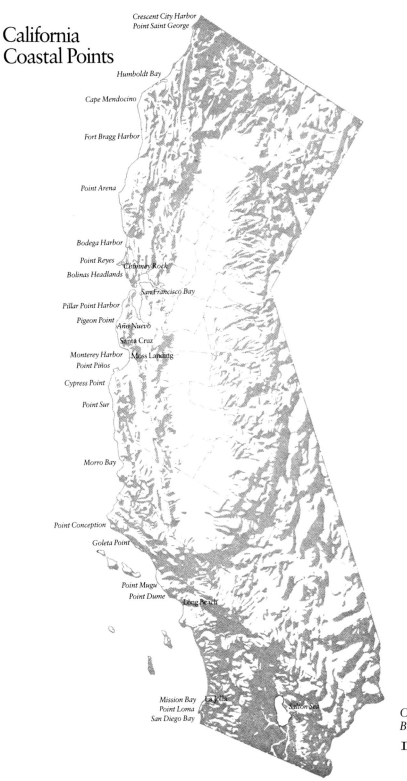

California
Coastal Points

Crescent City Harbor
Point Saint George

Humboldt Bay

Cape Mendocino

Fort Bragg Harbor

Point Arena

Bodega Harbor
Point Reyes   Chimney Rock
Bolinas Headlands
                San Francisco Bay
Pillar Point Harbor
Pigeon Point   Año Nuevo
               Santa Cruz
Monterey Harbor Moss Landing
Point Piños
Cypress Point

Point Sur

Morro Bay

Point Conception
Goleta Point

Point Mugu
Point Dume   Long Beach

Mission Bay   La Jolla
Point Loma   Salton Sea
San Diego Bay

waters, the center of the North Pacific Gyre is relatively still, warm, and lifeless. When arms of this "dead" water flow inshore, seabirds dependent on our normal eastern boundary current may find no food and face starvation (often the reason for die-offs, witnessed as numbers of beached birds).

Being part of the unpredictable ocean, the California Current is of course variable and unpredictable as well. During warm-water episodes or El Niños, upwelling is stifled, and resident bird species may fail in their breeding attempts because of food short-ages. Other bird species, though, more tropical in nature, may appear here in unusual numbers and combinations. Every fall the California Current slacks off because of the weakened winds, and warmer, subtropical water may wash toward our coast along with its attendant invertebrates, turtles, seabirds, and marine mammals. Every winter a countercurrent flows from the south to north. Such complex oceanography, in addition to coastal upwelling, makes life in the California Current exceedingly rich and varied.

Habitats of the Nearshore Pacific

Because of shifting currents, changing temperatures, variable winds, and tidal flush, surface habitats in the ocean — i.e., food sources — are irregular and cannot easily be pinned down or described. What can be talked about in the California nearshore Pacific, at least in a general way, are three distinct oceanic zones. Each one is consistent in the properties that make it different from the other two, and as different from the others as any such patches of land.

Northcoast Upwelling. Upwelling occurs when winds and/or currents cause circular and rising motions of water in the sea. One of the effects is that localized areas of very abundant food are created as krill is brought near the sea's surface. Ideal condi-tions to bring this force into play are a broad and irregular conti-nental shelf with mountains and canyons; isolated offshore escarpments or peaks; and a coast that lies nearly perpendicular to prevailing wind by which it is regularly pounded. This wind, especially in spring, drives the California Current harder and thus causes even more upwellings. The California Pacific from Point Conception north is a classic upwelling area, and under normal circumstances, marine, bird, and mammal life is relatively abun-dant. Much is known about the animals of this habitat.

Ocean Currents of the Northeast Pacific

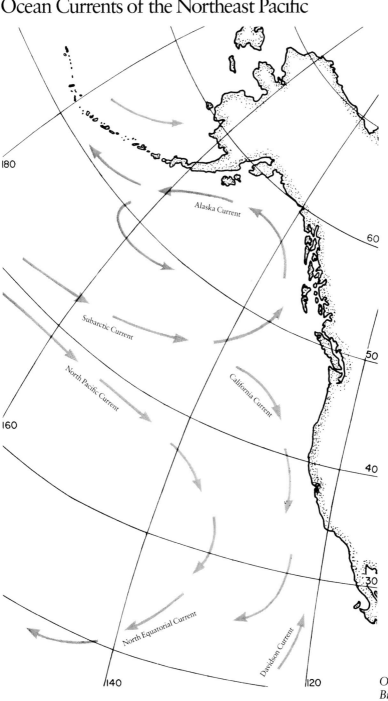

Alaska Current

Subarctic Current

North Pacific Current

California Current

North Equatorial Current

Davidson Current

180

160

140

120

60

50

40

30

The Southern California Bight. South of Point Conception, the coast breaks sharply back to the southeast, dissipating the clout of the northwest wind. This, in combination with the presence of the barrierlike Channel Islands that tame wild seas and the influence of warm, more tropical waters of Mexico, causes a bathtub effect making for very pleasant sailing but relatively poor wildlife observation. However, several kinds of birds, mammals, and especially turtles are much more easily found here than in colder areas, even those of great upwelling. Much is known about the animals of this habitat as well.

Central Pacific Waters: The Unknown Zone. Beyond the continental shelf, over the abyss of the deep blue sea, lie Central Pacific waters within the gyre. The water here is blue, because it is empty and sterile compared to grayer waters muddied by life, and fauna is scarce. Whereas above the continental shelf it is rare to be in a place where there are no animals, out in center of the gyre hours, even days, may pass without a single encounter with bird or mammal. It's a different world, bleak and desertlike. Animals are not numerous, and those present are especially adapted for locating sparse resources. Upwellings that bring food to the surface occur only above submarine mountains and valleys near enough to the surface to be affected by currents and wind wash. This is not the case in the very deep waters of the Central Pacific Gyre. Most of the animals that inhabit this zone are different from any seen near shore, and are seldom seen by humans. It is this habitat, far west of the continent, that remains poorly known to naturalists and biologists.

In this book we sometimes refer to this deep-water area beyond the continental shelf and 40 to 200 miles west of the coast as *the unknown zone.* Because of the logistical ease of one-day boat trips, inshore waters have been well explored for many years, and we now know the timing, status, and distribution (all subject to change as ocean conditions change) of birds occurring there. Birds present in the unknown zone, though, remain a virtual enigma. A few recent trips have shown that some southern *Pterodroma* petrels, such as Cook's and Murphy's (both unknown near California ten years ago), and some northern alcids, such as Horned Puffin and perhaps Parakeet Auklet, are regular and even common far offshore. As opportunities arise for us to investigate the unknown zone, its avifauna will

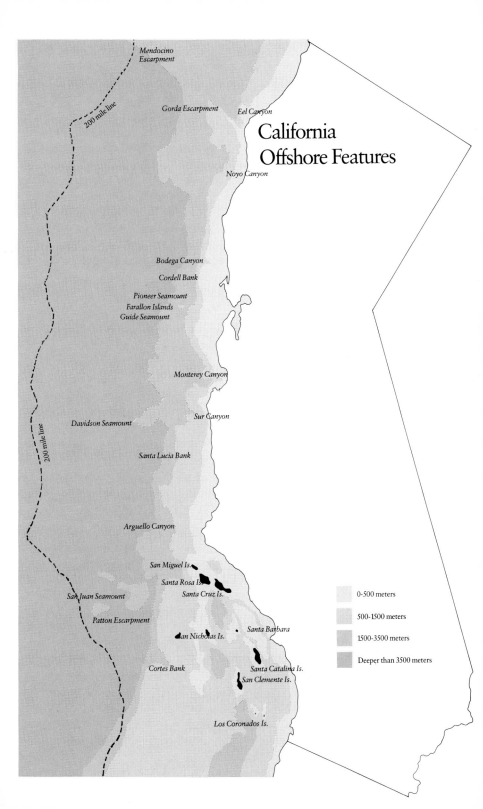

California
Offshore Features

Mendocino Escarpment

Gorda Escarpment

Eel Canyon

200 mile line

Noyo Canyon

Bodega Canyon

Cordell Bank

Pioneer Seamount
Farallon Islands
Guide Seamount

Monterey Canyon

Davidson Seamount

Sur Canyon

200 mile line

Santa Lucia Bank

Arguello Canyon

San Miguel Is.
Santa Rosa Is.
Santa Cruz Is.

San Juan Seamount

Patton Escarpment

San Nicholas Is.

Santa Barbara

Cortes Bank

Santa Catalina Is.
San Clemente Is.

Los Coronados Is.

0-500 meters

500-1500 meters

1500-3500 meters

Deeper than 3500 meters

eventually be sorted out, more species new to the nearshore Pacific will be found, and some birds now considered accidental will become predictable in their occurrence patterns. For now, however, and for well into the next century, the unknown zone all along the Pacific coast of North America remains its last ornithological frontier.

Taking a Pelagic Trip

Trips organized specifically to see pelagic birds are the first choice for nature lovers seeking closer kinship with ocean creatures, including marine mammals. Such trips usually provide excellent leadership and information about *all* animals encountered and, of course, are timed and oriented for maximum contact with wildlife.

Orientation. Most groups meet at the dock in the very early morning for departure. You will probably have been mailed a list of things to bring, but waterproof shoes or boots, *layers* of warm, wind- and waterproof clothes, gloves, and a hat that will stay on are essential if the area is known for spirited weather. Other basics include sunscreen (solar reflection is doubled at sea), seasickness remedies, food and drink, and binoculars (telescopes are useless).

Unless your group is entirely made up of veteran pelagic sailors who know exactly what to expect, your leader will gather everyone together before the boat leaves for a short orientation talk. Some basic rules of the sea will be covered, such as how to flush the head (toilet), where to throw up (only at the back railing), which places on the boat are off limits (like the top drive), and where smoking is permitted (if at all, only at the rear and away from other people). Since there are inherent dangers at sea, safety is a topic that will also be at least briefly addressed, if only to say where the life vests and rafts are and to suggest hanging on and helping each other.

Looking for Birds. Once you are under way, your leaders will be providing a running commentary on what birds and mammals are being seen and, when possible, some information about their biology, distribution, and features of identification. A fully functioning public address system is the most efficient way of passing news rapidly. Lacking this, the leaders will be running around a lot. (The loudspeakers scare sitting birds more than boat engines do, though, so the system will not be used when the boat is approaching flocks.) It is also nice to have occasional updates about where the boat is, the depth of the ocean, the future course, and probable changes in the condition of the sea (relative to the heading of the boat), especially if they contain good news.

Note that sometimes, even when there are birds or mammals in the area, the leaders may look like they aren't doing much (and, in fact, some of them are not). A few, however, are skilled enough at this that they can see what's coming and going all around the boat without really seeming to be looking at it.

Seeing. Many people look, few see. My friend Lone Bear, for many years a U.S. Forest Service fire lookout in the Sierra Nevada, never seemed to really *look* for fires. He was just there, going about the business of entertaining the Steller's Jays and chipmunks with jazz from his golden flute. He knew instantly, however, when a hunter struck a match two miles away . . . something was wrong in the woods. It is much the same with a skilled seabirder. Once you have looked often enough at the watery horizon to know when it is normal, you may see by sensing when there is something different, then pounce on it with binoculars while telling friends what and where it is.

To have a fulfilling wildlife experience on a pelagic trip, *each person* aboard should look for wildlife. The more one looks — scanning the horizon with binoculars, glancing skyward, or checking way back in the wake — the more different animals one will see. When mammals are present, they are generally much more easily seen than birds. Since dolphins and porpoises are often attracted to the boat to surf below the bow wave, and since many whales can be gently approached by experienced skippers, these animals often put on a close and exciting show.

Ocean birds are much smaller, of course, and many kinds are simply not attracted to boats. Other species are repelled by the noise (of the boat's motor and loud speaker). Thus the number of birds and species you see depends largely upon how much looking you are able to do.

Looking does not necessarily entail running around the boat, scanning 360 degrees. Some people do very well by picking a comfortable place to sit or lean and taking charge of that piece of the ocean pie they can see.

Picking a Spot on the Boat. Choosing the right spot to sit or stand during a pelagic trip is important. As the trip goes along, some choices are easily sorted out. For instance, if there is intense glare or drowning spray affecting one side, most people gravitate to the other. At the beginning, however, choices aren't so clear.

There are always some people who believe that more birds and mammals will be seen from the bow, will grab a spot there as soon as they get aboard, and will cling to that territory during the entire cruise. This works, sometimes. The trouble with the bow on most of the boats we have used is one of space. There is only room *on the rail* for a small number of people. Behind this first layer of bodies, everyone else trying to glimpse bits of water must peek between hats and hoods. Also behind the bow rail there is no support except for other people on all sides, so when the sea is rolling, the group on the bow sways around together like eel grass during ebb tide.

The very back of the boat may be worse! Not only is it where people who smoke, smoke, but on the fishing boats, it's also where the exhaust swirls. If that's not enough to do you in, the stern is the place where someone is often carving up raw squid, and, of course, there's usually someone throwing up.

Nope, it's the middle of these small boats that is best. There are good chances to see animals fore, aft, and off the sides, and because it's the boat's center of gravity, the middle is more stable than either end. It is also where there are often a few seats, and it is the driest area, spraywise.

Pinpointing a Sighting: Clock Direction. The easy way to get everyone to look in the same direction, even when the person speaking cannot be seen, is to think of the boat as a clock. Directly ahead of the bow (the pointed end) is 12 o'clock, and directly behind the stern is 6 o'clock. When you are facing forward, directly off the right side is 3 o'clock and directly left is 9 o'clock. Thus, to look for something at 5 o'clock, you look just to the left of straight back.

Occasionally, though, when a rare animal appears and excitement overrides composure, some of us can no longer distinguish 7 o'clock from 5 o'clock or 11:30 from 1:30. To remedy this problem, after many years of scientific research and deep thought, we have developed a fail-safe alternative: the *scream-and-point method*. It is a mere variation on the proven favorite "Thar she blows," but lacking a crow's nest, the drawback is that everyone needs to see which way the screamer is pointing.

After (or while) establishing direction, several other clues

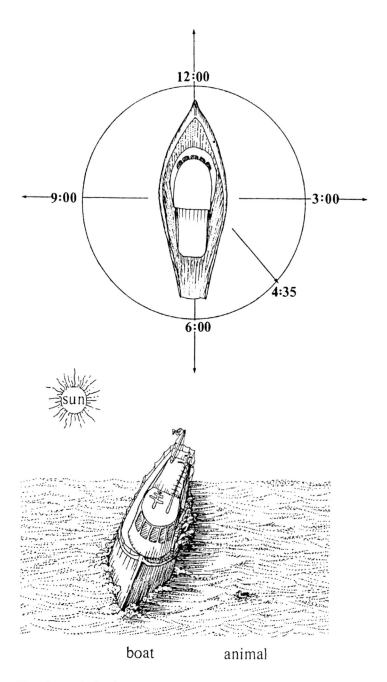

boat   animal

Top: *"Boat clock," for describing direction of an animal at sea.*
Bottom: *For best viewing, the boat is brought broadside to the*
object of interest. For best lighting, the boat is positioned
between the sun and the animal. (Ane Rovetta)

should be rapidly spoken. What the animal is doing, how far away it is, what it is with, flying left or right, and above or below the horizon: these will help pinpoint the object for others. For example, "At 3 o'clock, sitting on the water, behind the fulmar, two football fields away" or, "Jaeger, flying left past 11 o'clock at 100 yards, above the horizon, below the horizon, going away, behind a wave, now 9 o'clock, above the horizon, below the horizon . . . forget it." Things happen fast, and most passengers miss a lot, but accurate play-by-play directions will increase the overall success.

A Note to Leaders. Skippers who regularly take bird- or mammal-watching groups out know how to maneuver boats for best wildlife viewing, but new ones need some constructive instruction. First, the leaders should introduce themselves and make friends. Explain what the goals of the trip are, suggest a route, and ask if the skipper feels it is a good one. When the time is right, suggest how to approach animals in or on the water — slowly! Make sure the skipper understands that stationary animals are best viewed from either *side* of the boat (not head on, as then only those on the bow can see) and, when possible, from the side opposite the sun or glare, for best lighting. For smooth operations, the skipper should take instructions only from the leader and should know not to take it personally when the leader screams at him.

Chumming. Because a boat is but a tiny dot on the sea, unless it happens to be in a zone of concentrated natural feeding, chances of intercepting many of the birds present in the general area are small. Baiting (chumming) them to the boat increases the likelihood of seeing a much larger percentage of birds nearby.

There are two basic strategies: one is the all-day gull parade; the other is the organic oil slick.

The all-day gull-parade strategy teases a flock of large gulls into following the boat throughout the cruise, thereby attracting other, unusual bird species, such as albatrosses, shearwaters, fulmars, jaegers, skua, and small gulls and terns. These birds see the gull flock and hear their squealing feeding-frenzy calls. Though many will not stay long, most make a pass to examine the dimensions of the bounty. Good chum for the gull parade is anything gulls will eat (they are not too particular), that will float, and that may be carried on the boat in large quantity. Popcorn can be bought already popped in large bags at supermarkets (gulls like buttered rather than plain but hate cheese-flavored)

Other good choices are breakfast cereals (especially prized if mixed with animal grease), white bread (gulls are not too interested in high fiber content and often spit out what we call health food), chopped suet, crackers, pretzels, cupcakes, and Twinkies. If you are worried about what is good for them, forget it. If it will pass through their bodies without scratching anything, it is good for them. At dumps, favored items of these same gulls may be chicken bones and swizzle sticks. Usually chum is provided by the trip organizer, but there never seems to be enough, so each person may bring some (a loaf of bread) if it is convenient.

The organic-oil-slick strategy is quite different, and if it is attempted, materials will be provided by the trip organizer. On 27 August 1983, Terry Wahl, Bill Tweit, and I were 40 miles west of Westport, Washington, with a boatload of birders. The trip was going great, the water was glassy, and there were lots of birds. Four working shrimp trawlers were accompanied by over 5,000 shearwaters of five species, and we had seen Fork-tailed Storm-Petrels and several alcids on the way out. It was still quite early in the day, and Terry said, "Shall we go out to albatross habitat?" Sure! So we left this area of teeming activity, put the bow on the compass's big green W, and powered west. Birdlife promptly declined, and there was only the odd Sooty Shearwater to be seen. When we got to about 50 miles, there wasn't even that. I did a 360-degree scan. Nothing. Nothing but water, and Bill and Terry said, "This is the spot. Stop the engines." Passengers were glancing at each other in wonder as gloppy, smelly, clear liquid bloop-blooped from plastic bottles, clinging to itself in patches, floating on the surface of the sea. I scanned. Nothing. Then, at a great distance, a wheeling albatross! Within ten minutes there were 61 Black-footed Albatrosses sitting near the boat, a Long-tailed Jaeger circled near by, and two Tufted Puffins came roaring in like spiraling, black footballs and splashed to stops. Sabine's Gulls and storm-petrels appeared from nowhere. Everyone was impressed.

It doesn't always work this way, but it sure is worth trying when conditions are right. Right conditions seem to be deep water, light breezes, and calm seas. The liquid needs only to behave like oil and smell like death. Some people swear by shark liver oil, others swear at it. Even tuna oil works, squeezed from the can, but then if you like dolphins, you should be boycotting tuna. Unrefined cod liver oil is thought by some professionals to be the absolute best. It costs more than $100 per gallon, but a large, very attractive slick can be set with only a cupful. Try a variety and see what works best in your piece of ocean. When the birds arrive, feed them some gull chum to keep them around.

Looking for Ocean Birds from Shore

For people who dislike boats or are physically unable to ride on them, there are excellent seabirding alternatives. Equipped with a knowledge of key coastal promontories and the timings of migration, with the tenacity to endure some long sessions behind a telescope, with warm clothes, a bottle of eyedrops (and, for some, a wee bottle of brandy), and some luck, one will eventually see most of the regularly occurring species.

Because of daily bird movement and the optimal light conditions, morning on our coast is generally best. Migratory movement also occurs in the late afternoon, when the northwest wind sometimes moves birds nearer to shore. For afternoon watching, a high overcast is helpful in reducing the glare.

Birds that might be seen vary, depending upon the season and locality. From La Jolla, San Diego County, Black-vented Shearwaters are routinely seen in late fall and early winter, sometimes in large numbers (12,000 on 19 November 1979). Tufted Puffins would be exceptional there but are easily seen at islets where they nest, just off the headlands of Humboldt and Del Norte counties, from May through July (a place and time of no chance for Black-vented Shearwater).

The fall (July through October) is the overall best time, because there are more individual birds of a larger variety of species, and because the weather is generally good. During this period, from one of the better viewing stations (like Point Piños, Monterey County), several species of shearwaters and alcids, a couple of jaegers, small gulls, and perhaps a storm-petrel or two might be identified in a single watching session. Looking from the same spot on another day with similar conditions, the list total might be two cormorants and a starling. Don't get discouraged. Be persistent, and go again and again.

Spring migration is shorter than fall migration, and a sea watch might produce some large numbers of birds in fancy plumage (e.g., loons, brant, Sabine's Gulls, and phalaropes) but fewer truly pelagic species. Barry Sauppe and Peter Metropulos have shown, through thousands of hours of watching, that Pigeon Point, San Mateo County, is sometimes exceptionally productive during April and early May.

Winter is the time to look for Short-tailed Shearwater, Northern Fulmar, six species of alcids, and Black-legged Kittiwake.

In summer (June through August), millions of Sooty Shearwaters swarm nearshore and a Black-footed Albatross might be seen beyond. In the northern two-thirds of the state, Common Murres and Pigeon Guillemots nest on shore and near shore, and north of San Francisco, Tufted Puffins and Rhinoceros Auklets may be seen near some coastal points and islets.

Strategy. Looking for seabirds from shore takes discipline and special skill. One's equipment must be clean and working smoothly, especially the tripod.

Two or more people together are more efficient than one, and the group should be split between scopers and binocular-holding spotters. While the scopers scan the horizon for distant flying birds, the spotters look for swimming birds, otters, and high-flying jaegers.

Usually, most of the flying birds are going in one direction. The most proficient scoper will begin at the end of where they are *going* and work back. This gives that person a chance to rapidly identify a bird, "lead it" in the scope, quickly dive out of the way, and hope the next person, leaping to look, is able to pick up on the right one.

Wind. Sometimes strong west or northwest winds are very helpful in blowing certain offshore species to beaches, sheltered bays, or harbors. At other times, gusterly winds are simply obnoxious. There is usually some way to get to a calm spot. Try hiding behind a rock or a tree, or when possible (as it is in many places), position your parked car and watch out of the leeward windows.

Optics. Binoculars of eight to ten power are best. Lower power may fall short of distant birds and greater power are hard to hold still in a stiff breeze.

For scanning through telescopes, low-power eyepieces (15x to 22x) will be best, allowing a large field of view and maximum light. Greater power, however, may be necessary to pin down a tricky identification. A 15x to 60x zoom scope may be good, even though zoom scopes are not yet technically perfect; available light and sometimes focus weaken as power increases. The new, straight-eyepiece Kowa scopes are excellent, and though more difficult to master, Questar is the best. Bogen tripods with fluid heads are very good, currently the best. Car window mounts are available and easy to use.

Places. Following is a list of coastal viewing points, given from south to north: La Jolla, Point Fermin, Point Dume, Point Mugu (closed — military), Goleta Point, Point Sur, Point Piños, Pigeon Point, Bolinas Head, Point Reyes, Bodega Head, Point Arena, and Point Saint George. You may find others.

Ocean Trips and How to Find Them

A large number and fine variety of half- or whole-day boat trips off the coast are available and easy to find. They range from those that provide excellent leadership on large, fast vessels into known productive areas to fishing trips on which birders or whale-watchers can only hope for a good sighting (and hope they will know what it is if they see it). Pelagic birding trips are invariably more productive for observing seabirds and marine mammals than are any other kind of offering, including whale-watching trips. While there *are* good whale-watching trips, the naturalists and skipper are often the only people aboard who are *looking* for wildlife, and all too often that wildlife is limited to whales and porpoises.

On well-organized birding trips, in addition to the leaders and skipper, almost everyone on board is armed with excellent binoculars that they know how to use, and they have had such adventures before. Simply put, the more people actively looking, the more critters will be seen. Since birds are often present where mammals are feeding, and since cetaceans are so wonderful to be with, birding boats will deviate from their course to visit any whales or porpoises in the area. On a pelagic birding trip, as well as having the best birding experience possible, one's chances of close encounters with marine mammals are also at their highest.

Most trips are on chartered fishing boats that are rather small but very seaworthy, with heads (toilets) and covered storage for gear but precious little else to comfort the adventurer. With waterproof clothes, dry binoculars, and a bag of food, the adventure itself will provide the comfort.

At the present time, ocean trips available to the public in the nearshore Pacific are limited to a single day's duration. Only scientific research biologists are gifted with longer cruises. One-day trips, however, can be very productive and unforgettable outings.

In some areas, such as Monterey, California, where the continental shelf cuts within 4 miles of Point Piños and a major subaquatic canyon provides surface nutrients due to upwellings, many species of birds and mammals may be found during trips of just a few hours and within 5 miles of the coast. In other places like Westport, Washington, a rather long ride (40 miles) to nutrient-rich waters causes trips to be long in duration but, if the weather is acceptable, well worth the commute.

Following is a list of organizations that have offered top-quality ocean trips for wildlife observation for many years. All are enthusiastically recommended. For brochures, send them a self-addressed, stamped envelope, or call.

Shearwater Journeys. Debra Shearwater, P.O. Box 1445, Soquel, CA 95073; 408-688-1990. Debra is in her twelfth year of offering the best menu of pelagic wildlife voyages in the world. Being based at Monterey Bay (the single best place on the whole coast) doesn't hurt, but Debra's careful planning, friendly communication, recruitment of top leaders, and large offerings (over 40 trips in 1990) to different destinations make for an unbeatable attraction. The Monterey trips usually encounter a greater variety of ocean birds than any others in the North Pacific.

Westport, Washington. Terry Wahl, 3041 Eldridge, Bellingham, WA 98225; 206-733-8255. For over 20 years, Terry has been organizing pelagic trips from Westport west to Gray's Canyon and beyond. A fine leader, Terry is often accompanied by Bill Tweit and other experienced leaders, all excellent naturalists and teachers. The trip is usually nine to ten hours long, since the best wildlife areas are 35 to 50 miles offshore, but the fast boat makes the travel seem short. For a place this far north, reliability of trip completion from May into October is exceptional, with less than a 5% cancellation record due to weather. Terry does lead winter trips but seldom advertises them because the chance of being "weathered out" at that season is so high. The bird list for each trip is long and varied, and in 159 trips the Westporters have usually found Fork-tailed Storm-Petrel and have *never missed* Black-footed Albatross. Chances of seeing Flesh-footed Shearwater here are probably the best anywhere in our near-shore Pacific.

Western Field Ornithologists. c/o Ginger Johnson, 4637 Del Mar Avenue, San Diego, CA 92107; 619-223-7985. WFO runs two or three superb and inexpensive trips per year in the near-shore Pacific out of Mission Bay (San Diego), most to the vicinity of San Clemente Island. The large and comfortable vessels and usually calm water combine to make for very pleasant days of sailing, even if wildlife is relatively scarce. In fall, chances of seeing Black-vented Shearwater, Least Storm-Petrel, and Craveri's Murrelet are as good or better than anywhere else in nearshore waters north of Mexico, and Red-billed Tropicbirds were, at least formerly, regular. Leaders are always expert birders. On some trips, though, you may have to figure out the mammals by yourself.

Los Angeles Audubon Society. Attn. Pelagic Trips, LAAS, 7377 Santa Monica Boulevard, West Hollywood, CA 90046; 213-876-0202 (Tues-Sat); phone message with birding information, 213-874-1318. L.A. Audubon runs trips to Santa Barbara Island, then often south 10 miles to Osborne Banks. Though not expecting the number or variety of bird and mammal life found in upwelling areas north of Point Conception, these trips routinely find lots of exciting wildlife. Cetaceans often include Risso's, Pacific Bottlenose, and two varieties of Common dolphin. The trips also prowl very close to the island, where rocky shorebirds and various other coastal waterbirds and pinnipeds may well be seen. Of five trips offered in 1990 and scattered through the seasons, one on 22 September heads "out to sea as far as possible near San Nicolas Island." This is *toward* the area where several "blue water" species (Band-rumped and Wedge-rumped stormpetrels, Murphy's and Kermadec petrels, and others) have recently been churned up by ornithologists surveying from research vessels. Leaders listed, in differing combinations, include Kimball Garrett, Arnold Small, Herb and Olga Clark, and Jonathan Alderfer, all good ones.

Portland Audubon Society. Audubon House, 5151 NW Cornell Road, Portland OR 97210; 503-292-6855. Trips depart from Tillamook Bay, Oregon, and most go 15 to 20 miles offshore and are of seven hours' duration. Weather cancellations are not uncommon, so each scheduled trip has a back-up date the following weekend. If you're lucky, the first date will be canceled, and you'll have to spend a week roaming beautiful Oregon before you get to sea.

Whale-Watching Trips

Most of the larger charter-fishing companies along the coast have enthusiastically responded to people's demand to go whale-watching. These trips are organized by the charter offices at various harbors and are usually narrated by the boat's skipper. Some will be very informative, and some will be otherwise, but they offer good chances to get offshore. Most of these trips set out to see members of the large and growing California Gray Whale population during its migration season from Arctic waters to calving "pools" along the west coast of Baja California, and then back. The whales' passage happens from December into April, with a lull in the middle of that period for nursery school.

Gray Whales migrate very close to shore (more so in spring than fall) and can be seen well from points of land, but getting on a boat provides a more personal and exciting experience. Since the trips are in winter and close to shore, the bird list will be limited, but it might include Northern Fulmar, Pomarine Jaeger, Black-legged Kittiwake, Common Murre, and Rhinoceros Auklet. Many others are possible. Fall and winter trips to look for "great whales" like humpbacks and blues will go farther offshore and will be far more productive bird-wise than Gray Whale tours. If you find a trip seeking Sperm Whale, the avian possibilities are wide open.

Whale-watching trips available through professional organizations go specifically to view cetaceans (whales and porpoises) and pinnipeds (seals and sea lions). There are usually at least two experienced naturalists on board to spot, identify, describe, and interpret behavior of the animals seen. Although most of these naturalists will know the identity of most of the ocean birds, birds are definitely secondary objects unless, of course, there are no mammals to be found. Again, pelagic birding trips are more productive (given equal conditions) for observing seabirds and marine mammals than any other kind of offering, including whale-watching trips.

Whale-watching companies have hatched out all along the coast, and the quality of these outings certainly will have a wide range. Two organizations based in Central California are well known for their professionalism and their highly educational and delightful outings.

Shearwater Journeys. Debra Shearwater, P.O. Box 1445, Soquel, CA 95073; 408-688-1990. Although most of the ocean trips on Debra's schedule are listed as seabird journeys, she and most of her leaders have a keen interest in and love for cetaceans and pinnipeds. She lists marine mammal trips (which also seek birds), but whatever they are called, Shearwater Journeys are superb and complete adventures for all-round naturalists.

Ocean Birds

33

Oceanic Society Expeditions, Inc. Fort Mason Center, Building E, San Francisco, CA 94123; 415-474-3385. OSE, a nonprofit education and research organization, runs numerous winter Gray Whale trips from Half Moon Bay. In summer and fall there is a schedule of weekly Farallon Island trips. These are excellent, general, marine nature cruises that usually find Blue Whales or Humpbacks or both. Farallon trips provide close-up views of the islands themselves. Naturalists on board are very knowledgeable and good teachers. In addition to knowing all about mammals and oceanography, most are also field ornithologists who will very much welcome anyone mostly interested in birds to the trip.

Fishing Trips for Birds and Mammals

Most large harbors along the coast offer daily party boat fishing trips. You can simply call the local companies to learn availability, prices, departure times, and other details. Because these boats only go fishing, you may wish to buy a license and, during periods of slow bird activity, catch your dinner — or dinner for 20 friends.

In choosing a fishing trip to look for marine vertebrates, it is very important to know where the boat is going or at least what kind of fish are targeted. Tuna trips, especially for albacore or bonito, are usually best, because these fish live in deep water and are usually at warm spots or in warm currents. Orcas, Pilot Whales, and Risso's and smaller dolphins are often nearby. Salmon trips often travel nearer shore, but because trolling is the fishing strategy, the boat keeps moving and will cover more territory. Rockfish trips require more thinking, because rockfish are sought in two basic habitats — in shallows very near the coast, and at underwater ridges or mountains, some well offshore. The first choice could be pretty boring unless you like to watch Sanderlings from the wet side, and the second choice could be wildly exciting, since many fine birds and mammals are attracted to upwellings (as well as to bits of dead fish).

Ferry Boats

Ferry rides from Anacortes, Washington, through the San Juan Islands to Sidney, British Columbia, on Vancouver Island, and also from Tsawassen, B.C., to Sidney, can be

Long-tailed Jaegers (p. 117). Top: subadult. Note that elongate central tail feathers are rounded during early growth. (Mike Danzenbaker) Bottom: adult, lacking long central tail feathers. Note two white-shafted primaries and black trailing edge to gray dorsal wing. (David Leal)

very good for birds in season, especially alcids. The Blackball Transport ferry from Victoria, B.C., to Port Angeles, Washington, crossing the Strait of Juan de Fuca, may be even better, because, in addition to alcids, a few shearwaters, fulmars, or jaegers may be found. The problem is that the ships are huge and the observer is high above the water. The operators are Washington State Ferry System, 801 Alaskan Way, Seattle, WA 98104, 800-542-0810 (or in Seattle 464-6400); British Columbia Ferry Corporation, 1112 Fort Street, Victoria, B.C., V8V 4V2, 604-386-3431; and Blackball Transport, Inc., 10777 Main, Bellevue, WA 98004, 206-622-2222. Reservations are necessary.

A large number of ferry routes are offered by Alaska Marine Highway, Box R, Juneau, AK 99811; 800-642-0066. All of these trips are superb for viewing wildlife, often with awesome scenic backdrops. A couple of the most productive routes for birds are Homer to Dutch Harbor (three days with stops at Kodiak and Cold Bay) and Homer to Seward (about one and a half days with a stop at Kodiak). Both encounter huge numbers of ocean birds, with chances for Mottled Petrel and Aleutian Tern and, between Cold Bay and Dutch Harbor, Laysan Albatross and the rare and local Whiskered Auklet. These trips require a lot of planning. Make sure the current schedule crosses the best areas during daylight hours. Reservations are necessary.

In Southern California, there are several ferry trips each day from Long Beach *and* San Pedro to Avalon on Santa Catalina in the Channel Islands. The crossing takes only about one hour but runs through very good ocean bird habitat where shearwaters, phalaropes, jaegers, alcids, and cetaceans may be seen when the season is right (August through October and mid-March through May). When the season is wrong you'll probably have a really good time anyway. In addition to shops, restaurants, and other tourist attractions, Santa Catalina has an interesting fauna of its own and during migration periods is a magnet for misoriented landbirds. The boats themselves are large, fast, and single-minded about the commute, but if your time is limited, they offer a pleasant way to get offshore. Call Catalina Cruises, 213-547-1162, or Catalina Channel Express, 800-257-2227.

Tubenoses

Tube-noses is the common term for all members of this
order, which includes albatrosses, shearwaters, petrels, fulmars,
and storm-petrels. All can drink and desalt seawater. The thick,
saline impurities are excreted from special tubes on the dorsal
ridge of the bill or through specially designed nostrils. Birds in
this group are truly oceanic and, away from nesting localities,
never willingly go to land.

Albatrosses. Family Diomedeidae

Depending upon which taxonomy one follows, there are 14
to 16 albatross species in the world. Five of these have been documented as occurring in the nearshore Pacific. Albatrosses (even
the "small" ones) are huge birds with extremely long and narrow
wings. Magnificent in flight, they use wind and lift from waves
to hurtle themselves on set wings through the swells, over the
crests, and up into wheeling, high, slicing arcs. The flight of the
albatross must be seen to be believed.

Away from nesting islands, albatrosses are entirely oceanic,
feeding on offal, carrion, garbage from ships, and surface
organisms such as small fish and squid. Contrary to what is
often published about these birds not following ships, most
albatross species are easily lured to active fishing trawlers or
ships baiting for birds with chum.

Wandering Albatross
(Diomedea exulans)

There is only one record for our region. A subadult female
was photographed sitting on a bluff at Sea Ranch,
Sonoma County, on 11 and 12 July 1967. Though the
sighting was not confirmed in life by ornithologists, photos of
the unwary bird taken by surprised local residents are excellent
and unambiguous. When a westerly breeze came up later, on

*Ocean
Birds*

37

Wandering Albatross (p. 37). Top: *adult.* Bottom: *young.*
(Alan McBride)

the twelfth, the great bird flew seaward and was not seen again. Though its appearance here might have been the result of a human assist, it may just as well have been the natural occurrence of a lost or adventuresome individual. Having been accepted by the California Bird Records Committee, this is one of very few records of the species ever encountered in the Northern Hemisphere and is the only record for the entire Northeast Pacific. Wandering Albatross is an abundant circumpolar, Southern Hemisphere species.

Identification. Like the slightly more expected Short-tailed Albatross, this is a huge bird (wingspan up to 12 feet!) that makes our regular albatrosses (Black-footed and Laysan) seem small. Separation from Short-tailed after the earliest plumage stages certainly presents an identification problem. If Short-tailed or one of the great southern (Wandering and Royal) albatrosses is ever encountered here, as many photographs as possible should be taken, augmented with field sketches and written descriptions that precisely document every aspect of the bird, with particular focus on the pattern of the upperwing, back, tail, head, and bill.

Notes. Wandering Albatrosses do not nest until they are over nine years old and then only breed every two years. Adults share in preparation of the nest, with the male bringing material and the female doing construction. Both take part in incubation and care of the single youngster. The incubation period averages about 75 days, with parents trading off every 2½ weeks. The fledgling period is about 275 days, bringing the whole nesting cycle to about 11 months. This is not your average bird!

Short-tailed Albatross

(Diomedea albatrus)

Now extremely rare. Formerly (before 1900), Short-tailed Albatrosses were common very near the West Coast of North America, even regularly entering San Francisco Bay. More recently, there are less than 20 records in the whole Northeast Pacific in the last 80 years, but the outlook is bright for more in the future. Any at-sea sighting in the Eastern Pacific should be considered a mammoth event, and all photographic, artistic, and written documentation should be attempted.

Short-tailed Albatross (p. 39). Top: "adolescent" third or fourth plumage. (Mike Wihler) Bottom left and right: first flying plumage. (Don Roberson, left; Rich Stallcup, right)

Identification. Because of its large size and obvious relationships, the Short-tailed Albatross resembles the giant southern albatrosses (Wandering and Royal) much more than it does our regular species (Black-footed and Laysan); the latter are small by comparison. Different from Laysans, adult Short-taileds have white backs, huge white patches on the dorsal innerwings, and all-white underwings. Laysans have dark backs and entirely dark dorsal wings (except for a few white-shafted primaries), and the underwings have various amounts of black intruding into the white from the black leading edges. Very young Short-taileds, while all brown like Black-footeds, are darker birds, especially about their heads, which are blackish and which strikingly enunciate their massive, bubble-gum pink bills. Short-taileds have pink legs, feet, toes, and webs. Black-footeds have *black* bills, legs, feet, toes, and webs. Old and worn Black-footeds may become very pale, and their bills may become whitish or straw-colored. The bills of both Laysan and Black-footed albatrosses are dinky compared to that of the larger Short-tailed.

The real identification problem would be with the Wandering or Royal albatross, and since Wandering has occurred (once), it must be considered. Wanderings are even bigger than Short-taileds, but a solitary bird would be a hard call against an immense background like the sky or the Pacific Ocean. The plumage sequences that both species go through are similar but separable when an observer knows what bits of anatomy to concentrate on. For young birds, these bits would be face, crown, nape, inner dorsal wing, and underwing. Wanderings have white underwings throughout their flying life, whereas Short-taileds' underwings are dark until the body becomes mostly white. For adults, the bits of anatomy to concentrate on are head color, nuchal (neck) markings, wing pattern, and markings (or lack of them) on the pink bill.

Behavior. A juvenile at Cordell Bank on 3 November 1985 came in and landed with Black-footed Albatrosses near our boat and picked at popcorn and sandwiches thrown to it. It stayed for 20 minutes. The same bird was found again in the same area two days later. Another juvenile on 7 December 1988, about 270 miles southwest of Point Sur, was picking at a dead giant squid. "The combination seemed appropriate; perhaps giant squid, one of which could keep a big albatross happy for weeks, is a primary food source" (Peter Pyle).

Black-footed Albatross (p. 43). Top: dorsal view. (Mike Danzenbaker) Inset: pale-headed individual. (Rod Norden) Middle: ventral view. (Rod Norden) Bottom: close-up. (Paul Crawford)

Notes. The Short-tailed Albatross was very nearly exterminated due to killings on its breeding grounds, 600 miles south
of Japan, during the early part of this century. Some say the
slaughter was for the birds' yellow-gold head feathers (to fan-
cify human clothing), but probably it was also for food and
perhaps for "sport." The fact that young birds do not return to
the homeland for several years is what saved the species from
extinction. After people stopped pounding away at the colonies
because the small numbers or absence of birds made it no longer
profitable, the young albatrosses returned to nest for the first
time. The species was thought to be extinct after World War II,
but 10 pairs were found back on Torishima Island in 1954 and
their numbers have steadily increased. In 1971, 12 individuals
were found at Minamiko-jima, and by 1982, 50 pairs were estimated. Nesting grounds and possible nesting grounds are now
either rigidly protected or inaccessible. The world population of
Short-tailed Albatrosses, though slowly increasing, may still be
less than 300 birds.

Black-footed Albatross
(Diomedea nigripes)

This is the most common albatross to be found in nearshore California waters. It is more often recorded—and
is found in larger numbers—off the northern part of the
state, especially after August, but individuals may appear anywhere offshore at any time of year. They are concentrated over
the continental shelf, which varies from 4 to more than 100 miles
wide. During the species' peak presence offshore from mid-May
through mid-August, many individuals are likely to be found on
any day. Unfortunately, they are usually absent from Monterey
south from mid-August through November, the period when
most birding boats are scheduled and when the greatest ocean
bird diversity graces our shore.

    Identification. With seven-foot wingspans and a mastery of
aerodynamic flight, even these "small" albatrosses are always
thrilling to see. They are mostly uniform dark brown, with several white-shafted primaries, white feathers around the base
of the black bill, and white undertail (and sometimes uppertail)
coverts. The legs and feet are black. Old or worn birds may
become very pale on the belly and underwings, and such individ-

uals have caused a rush of excitement for some anxious birders. The huge, very rare Short-tailed Albatross is *all* dark brown (blackish on the head) when young, with pinkish legs and feet and a humongous pink bill. In short, Black-footed Albatrosses are very distinctive. Even so, the bird most often misidentified as one, offshore and distant, is . . . Brown Pelican! Many are the keen birders who have been taken in by the charade; who would like to be next?

Behavior. Black-footed Albatrosses are easily attracted to boats by chumming, so when they're present, everyone gets a good view and a photograph. In season, albatrosses may escort boats for miles and hours at a time. They are scavengers, feeding on a variety of dead things (they love squid), and will follow large ships for days to harvest leftovers from the crew's mess.

Notes. The Black-footed Albatross nests mostly in the northwest Hawaiian Islands, with scattered colonies west to Torishima.

Laysan Albatross
(Diomedea immutabilis)

Rather rare nearshore (Laysans become more common offshore up to 200 miles), but in recent years this species has been found annually at various stations near the mainland. Increased searching at key spots (such as Cordell Bank) and an increase in winter bird trips may be partly responsible for more nearshore sightings. There may just be more birds. Laysans have recently made their debut as *nesting* birds in the Eastern Pacific (see *Notes,* below)! Unlike the much more common Black-footed Albatross, most records for Laysans are in the winter (but there are records for every month), from late October through February, and as many as ten have been observed on a single November day over Cordell Bank, 20 to 30 miles west of Point Reyes. In the Western Pacific, Laysans are known to avoid water that is warmer than 13° C (55.4° F).

Also unlike Black-footeds, Laysans are not concentrated on the continental shelf and will prove to be regular and perhaps common in Central Pacific waters more than 100 miles from the coast. On 8 December 1988, between 140 miles southwest of Point Arena and 74 miles west of Point Gorda, 45 Laysan Albatrosses were estimated by experienced observers. It was noted that during the day there were "seldom none in view." More and more distant bird surveys into the North American Pacific will revise distributional understanding as to the status of this species and will broaden its role as a member of California's pelagic fauna.

Identification. Patterned rather like an adult Western Gull but much larger, the Laysan Albatross is not likely to be mistaken for any other regularly occurring bird. Adult Short-tailed Albatrosses have white backs and dorsal innerwings, wholly white underwings, and are much more massive. Laysans have dark backs and entirely dark dorsal wings and are variously black and white on the underwings.

It is very likely that other small Southern Hemisphere albatrosses will be found here in the future (and probably have occurred here already but got away unnoticed), so do not assume that a bird of this sort is a Laysan. Identify each bird beyond question. Pay special attention to (1) the pattern of the underwings, (2) the facial expression and head color, and (3) the pattern and color of the bill. Take photographs, make sketches, and write down what you see at the time you see it. These birds are easily attracted to small boats chumming food scraps.

Notes. Most of the world's population breeds in the leeward Hawaiian chain and west to Bonin Island south of Japan, where the species has been expanding in range and population size in recent years. Startling is the fact that in the late 1980s Laysan Albatrosses were found *nesting* in the Eastern Pacific at Isla Guadalupe and at Isla Clarion in the Revillagigedo archipelago off Baja California. At Isla San Benedicto, also in the Revillagigedos, many Laysans were found courting in 1988, and though nesting could not be documented, it appeared imminent (*fide* Steve Howell and Sophie Webb).

Earlier in the eighties, Bob Pitman noted congregations around Alijos Rocks 185 miles west of southern Baja California. In January and April 1983, breeding displays were taking place, but actual nesting there has not been confirmed.

On 5 May 1976, a Laysan Albatross was seen at Morongo Pass, Riverside County. It was flying west over the desert, headed toward San Gorgonio Pass and the Pacific. Undoubtedly, this bird had become "trapped" in the north end of the Gulf of California, as were two other individuals in summer 1984: from 21 May to 20 June one remained in the north end of the Salton Sea.

Top: *Laysan Albatross (p.44), ventral view. (Peter Pyle)* Inset:
Laysan Albatross, dorsal view. (Peter LaTourette) Bottom: *White-
capped Albatross (p. 47). (Alan McBride)*

It was joined by a second bird on 9 June, and at times they were involved in courting behavior. Another Laysan hit a power line near Palm Springs, Riverside County, on 6 May 1985!

White-capped Albatross
(Diomedea cauta)

There is but one definite record off the west coast of North America, that being an adult female collected 39 miles west of the Quillayute River mouth, Grays Harbor County, Washington, on 1 September 1951. This is the only record for the North Pacific, and it could just as easily have occurred off California.

Identification. Huge, like Short-tailed Albatross, but in plumage more like Laysan. Adults are black-backed and have black upperwing surfaces and black tails. The underwing is wholly white, finely bordered on the leading and trailing edges with black. Where this leading edge meets the body there is a longer black "thumbmark" that reaches back slightly into the wingpit. Immatures are much like adults but have gray hoods (when very young) that fade with age to narrow gray nuchal collars. The White-capped's black thumbmark, along with its large size, should identify the species from all others in the world.

Notes. There are four other species of black-backed, white-bellied albatrosses, and any could reach the California Pacific. On at least one occasion, an albatross of this sort "with a gray head" was seen just outside Monterey Bay. It was of a kind as yet unknown in the North Pacific and remained unidentified. When one of these is found, pay careful attention to (1) the pattern of the underwings, (2) facial expression and head color, and (3) pattern and color of the bill. Take photos and make sketches.

The Washington bird was of the large, widespread subspecies *D. c. cauta*. It nests at Tasmania, the Bass Strait region of Australia, and Auckland Island, and many birds move easterly toward South America in April and May.

Of about 66 species worldwide, only 17 have been documented from the nearshore Pacific. Other species may soon be added as we more thoroughly investigate deep blue-water regions well offshore.

Flight behavior varies greatly among these medium-sized tubenoses, from the small, extremely fast "Cookilaria petrels" (Cook's, Stejneger's, Pycroft's, etc.) that fly like a "bat-outa-hell," to large shearwaters such as Pink-footed, whose slow flaps could be called lumbering. During periods of strong wind, similarities in their flight styles increase, and all members of the family boomerang around the rolling waves on stiff, set wings. Even the big shearwaters and fulmars then dash about like the smaller *Pterodroma* petrels.

Northern Fulmar
(Fulmarus glacialis)

Mostly a winter bird offshore California, abundant some years and scarce in others. Eruptions of abundance in early winter (October through December) are often followed by heavy mortality, evidenced by large numbers of emaciated beached corpses. Though fulmars are much more common offshore, during invasion years individuals may be seen at harbors waiting for scraps of fish, or from coastal points flying nearshore. Following invasion winters, individuals may be found throughout the next spring and into summer, but most summer birds are noticeably unhealthy and all may be, to some degree. Fulmars are generally more common and arrive earlier in Northern than in Southern California waters.

Identification. Shearwater-like in its size, its "tubed nose," and its stiff-winged flight. It is highly variable in plumage, from immaculate white to uniform dark gray, and can be anything in between, including variously mottled. Off California, medium-gray sorts usually outnumber all others at least eight to one, but rarely, white birds with gray mantles predominate. In all but the darkest birds, white-shafted primaries show as a white flash on the upper surface of the open wing. Differing from shearwaters, fulmars have large, round heads and thick, short, yellow bills. The wingtips appear more rounded on fulmars, and the white outerwing patches are unlike those of any shearwater (but do resemble those of some true petrels).

Behavior. Very competitive scavengers, fulmars are easily attracted to boats with a bird flock in tow; they will swim to chum quite close to the boat if the boat stops. Though many may be seen scattered about a feeding area, fulmars are not gregarious (as are shearwaters) and are often seen flying or sitting alone. When they do associate with other birds, it is often with gulls. They fly much like shearwaters do, usually clipping along quickly just above the waves, occasionally gliding between flaps. When the wind comes up, fulmars really show their stuff, wheeling and arcing at high speed, more like true petrels than shearwaters.

Notes. Unlike our other large tubenoses, Northern Fulmars nest in the *North* Pacific, on cliff faces or in shallow burrows on islands.

Mottled Petrel
(Pterodroma inexpectata)

Rarely encountered in the nearshore Pacific, doubtless more common (in season) over deep water. Five were found dead or dying on beaches (two in Marin County, two in San Luis Obispo County, and one in Humboldt County) in 1976 and 1977 during thorough beached-bird surveys by volunteers for the Point Reyes Bird Observatory. A few other individuals have been seen by observers on scientific cruises, well offshore, and there are two reports of birds seen from shore during strong west winds, one, off Point Mugu, Ventura County, California, on 30 December 1980, and one off Point Piños, Monterey County, on 12 December 1984. No clear chronology has yet emerged, but most records south of Alaska are for February-March, July-August, and November-December. Three Mottled Petrels were seen on 8 December 1988, 100 miles off Point Arena, and perhaps they are regular there in winter. Records from off southern Alaska, where the species is considered uncommon, span early spring to late fall. We saw seven along the deep-water route from Kodiak Island to Seward in early June 1977, but in the following six summers, nine crossings on the same route produced none. When seen from or near land, high onshore winds are usually responsible. Mottled Petrels nest only on islands off New Zealand, and much of the population is transequatorial, spending its at-sea time in the North Pacific.

Northern Fulmars (p. 48). Top: an Atlantic individual. Many North Pacific birds are similar. (Jack Swenson) Middle: gray phase. (Rich Stallcup) Bottom: a blotchy individual. (Rich Stallcup)

This bird was formerly called Scaled Petrel.

Identification. A medium-sized hunky *Pterodroma*. Strikingly patterned and, with a good view, *easy to identify!* Unlike most species that have at least one look-alike congener, this bird, given a decent view, is unmistakable. In size it is about one-third bigger than Cook's or Stejneger's petrel and a bit smaller than Northern Fulmar. Its upperparts are most like Cook's Petrel: a light gray cap, nape, back, and rump; a black smudge behind the eye; and a black open W pattern across the extended gray upperwings. The tail is gray, with some white in the outer tail feathers (not as much as in Cook's). The ventral pattern is much more distinctive, Mottled being the only *Pterodroma* with a *gray or blackish belly* sharply contrasting the white breast and white undertail coverts. In fresh plumage, the gray belly is very dark and obvious; wear causes it to pale and makes identification somewhat more difficult. The underwings are mostly bright white but are divided by a wide, striking black ulnar bar from the midaxillaries to the wrist and along the leading edge of the outerwing.

Solander's Petrel
(Pterodroma solandri)

There is no definite record from our area, but this species has been seen by experienced ocean birders in the North-Central Pacific in July and September and about 465 miles south-southwest of Point Conception on 6 December 1988. Most other records of "dark *Pterodromas*" off California probably were Murphy's Petrels (but there is a lot to be learned about the topic over the next decade or so). Most Solander's Petrels nest on Lord Howe Island, off eastern Australia, from June through November, so birds seen in the North Pacific at that time no doubt are nonbreeding wanderers. This species is also known as Providence Petrel or Bird of Providence.

Identification. This big petrel is the size of a Sooty Shearwater, which it superficially resembles. Clearly placing it in the *Pterodroma* category, though, are its blunt head, big thick bill, long and slightly wedge-shaped tail, and flight behavior. Its body plumage is entirely brown or gray-brown; it has a darker hood (seen from below), a blackish tail, and a striking white patch divided by a dark "comma" on the ventral side of the outerwing. The comma is caused by the presence of blackish *tips* on the white greater wing coverts. Solander's also has some white feathering on the forecrown and chin; this forms a grayish-white ring around the face at the base of the bill. Murphy's Petrels that show white flecking on the forecrown also show much white in the throat, often extending into the malar region.

On the water, facial pattern and head-bill proportions will be the best features separating Solander's and Murphy's petrels. Whereas Solander's has a relatively smaller, more squared head and a longer, deeper bill (30% bigger than Murphy's), Murphy's head is relatively larger and more rounded, emphasizing the smallness of its shorter, shallower bill. As a bird runs to take off, stare at the legs and feet. Solander's feet and webs are black; those of Murphy's are pinkish, black only on the distal webs.

Murphy's Petrel is the only real look-alike, but dark phases of other *Pterodromas,* especially Kermadec and Herald, should also be considered.

Behavior. Flight is typically *Pterodroma*-like, with much stiff-winged gliding and arcing, but "heavy." Arcing is relatively horizontal and drawn out compared to that of Murphy's Petrel, which is more rapid, vertical, and bouncy.

During gale-force winds (when everything flies like a *Pterodroma,* even *Velella), Pterodroma* fever sometimes becomes the birder's second most common infirmity over deep water. Then shearwaters, fulmars, and even Sabine's Gulls have been called petrels.

Murphy's Petrel
(Pterodroma ultima)

Absent over the shallows of the continental shelf and within 30 miles of land, but possibly regular (and even common) over deep, offshore habitats — at least during spring and early summer. During the past ten years there have been several sight records, well offshore, by experienced seabirders conducting pelagic censuses from research vessels. Except for two beached corpses in Oregon, though, no documentation (identifiable photos or specimens) was obtained, and the status of this hard-to-identify bird remained enigmatic until 1989. That year, on 29–30 April, an expedition was mounted specifically to clarify questions of dark *Pterodromas'* identification and distribution. *Ninety-eight* Murphy's Petrels were counted and undeniably documented from 32 to 90 miles west (west-southwest and west-northwest) of San Francisco. Many photographs were taken, and one specimen was collected about 85 miles west-southwest of Point Reyes. Except for the *113* Cook's Petrels counted on the same trip, these were the only *Pterodromas* found on the expedition.

Murphy's Petrels nest on islands in the South-Central Pacific, halfway between Australia and South America. Their breeding biology is poorly known, and their pelagic range away from nesting spots is poorly understood. From what we now know, it seems certain that this species and possibly the similar Solander's Petrel may be regular members of California's offshore fauna.

Identification. Very similar to Solander's Petrel, and like that species shows skill at concealing its most distinctive features. Smaller than Solander's, Murphy's is mostly a steely gray-brown in plumage. It has an obvious open M pattern of black across its extended gray upperwings, an obscure mark in Solander's. In Murphy's, the underwing pattern, though variable, tends to be as pale on the ventral innerwing (secondaries) as on the ventral outerwing (primaries). In Solander's, the ventral secondaries are dark, exaggerating the white blaze on the ventral primaries. Some Murphy's have a dark "comma" through the pale outerwing, formed by the webs of the greater coverts — not by their tips as in Solander's. In certain lighting conditions Murphy's may appear subtly dark-hooded from below but not as strongly so as Solander's. Like Solander's, Murphy's Petrels have white feathering on the chin, but it is more extensive, making most individuals appear "white-throated" — a look that Solander's lacks. Also, some Murphy's have a sprinkling of light feathers on the dark forecrown but not enough to make that area look whitish, as it does in Solander's. Murphy's throat always has more white feathering than does its forehead.

On the water (and possibly discernable in close flying views), facial pattern and head-bill proportions may be helpful in separating Murphy's and Solander's petrels. Whereas Murphy's has a relatively larger, more rounded head and smaller bill, Solander's head is smaller and more squared, and its bill is clearly larger and more bulbous. Try to see the legs and feet as one of these birds runs to take off or scratches itself. In Murphy's, they are pink, with black only on the distal webs. In Solander's, they are usually all black (rarely grayish with black tips). Solander's Petrel is the only real look-alike, but dark-phased Kermadec and Herald petrels should also be considered.

Top: *Mottled Petrel (p. 49), a beached casualty. (Point Reyes Bird Observatory)* Bottom: *Juan Fernandez Petrel. A number of ocean bird species that are part of the avifauna of the Northeast Pacific have not yet made a witnessed debut to the geographic area covered in this book. Near the top of that list of expected birds are Juan Fernandez Petrel (Pterodroma externa), shown here, and the similar Hawaiian Petrel (Pterodroma phaeopygia). (Peter Pyle)*

Ocean
Birds

54

Behavior. Flight is typically *Pterodroma*, with much rapid, stiff-winged gliding and arcing, but the arcing is high, bouncy, and vertical compared to the more horizontal style of Solander's.

During gale-force winds, shearwaters, fulmars, gulls, and even phalaropes fly like *Pterodromas*, and all have been accused of being petrels by overly enthusiastic observers.

Kermadec Petrel
(Pterodroma neglecta)

A single bird was very well seen and described on 7 December 1988, 248 miles west-southwest of Point Sur, California. "It was flying directly toward North American waters, where it has yet to be recorded" (Peter Pyle). Given the speed at which these things fly, it probably punctured the boundary of the United States within an hour after the sighting. There are also two reports of individual Kermadec Petrels between 100 and 200 miles off San Nicolas Island in January 1989 and February 1990 (*fide* Peter Pyle). The species is widespread in the Tropical Pacific (both sides) and ranges widely in the Central and North Pacific, except near coasts. During winter it is perhaps regular in small numbers over deep waters well offshore California and casual within the official bird boundary (200 miles) of the state.

Identification. There are dark ones, light ones, and intermediates. Kermadec Petrel is a large *Pterodroma* with jaegerlike wings that are long, pointed, and slightly crooked at the wrist. Typical of all individuals is a distinct white patch on the outward upperwing surface. Caused by the bright white shafts and basal webs to the primaries, these white flashes add to the species' jaegerlike appearance and are lacking in Murphy's and Solander's petrels.

Behavior. Kermadecs are typically *Pterodroma* in their flight style: rapid, blow-by, and stiff-winged. They also are sometimes aggressive toward other birds, and will chase other species until they surrender their food, fresh or otherwise (*fide* Larry Spear and David Ainley). These birds look like and sometimes act like jaegers.

Dark Pterodromas. Top: Kermadec Petrels (p. 55), ventral view (left) and dorsal view (right). Middle: Murphy's Petrels (p. 52), ventral views (left and middle), showing variation in underwing pattern, and dorsal view (right). Bottom: Solander's Petrel (p. 51), ventral view (left) and dorsal view (right). Note that Murphy's have more abrupt arcs in normal flight than do Solander's or Kermadec. (Keith Hansen)

Top: *Solander's Petrel (p. 51), off the east coast of Australia.*
(Alan McBride) Middle and bottom: *Murphy's Petrel (p. 52).*
(Mike Danzenbaker)

Cook's Petrel
(Pterodroma cookii)

A spring, summer, and fall visitor far offshore. As with all our *Pterodroma* species, the abundance status, distribution, and timing of Cook's Petrel here are just now beginning to be understood. At least 8 individuals were carefully identified around 100 miles west of Morro Bay between 7 October and 1 December 1979; others have been seen just west of Cordell Bank during June (5 on 23 June 1985); 1 was present at the north end of the Salton Sea (24–29 July 1984); and another was found dead on a Santa Cruz street on 17 November 1983. On an expedition on 29–30 April 1989, 113 Cook's were counted between 75 and 90 miles west of Point Reyes. Cook's Petrels nest on islands off New Zealand, and much of the population is thought to cross the Equator and spend at-sea time in the Eastern Pacific, as far north as the Aleutians, where it is of accidental occurrence. Clearer distribution boundaries are not well understood.

Identification. A very small gadfly petrel. Entirely white below, including most of the underwings. The upperparts are entirely light gray (including the head and nape), except for a brief black patch behind the eye and a black open W pattern across the extended wings, formed by black outer primaries and innerwing coverts. When seen, the white outer tail feathers boldly contrast the gray center of the dorsal tail.

Several very similar petrel species might occur well offshore California. Of those documented so far, Stejneger's and Mottled petrels are most similar to Cook's. Pycroft's Petrel may occur here, but because it looks so much like Cook's, it will require special documentation or new identification techniques to confirm. Subtle differences are Pycroft's smaller size, smaller bill, slightly darker crown (when fresh), and relatively broader underwing carpal bar.

Though the Santa Cruz specimen was definitely *P. cookii* and the other sightings were thought to be, Cook's sibling species *P. defilippiana*, called Masatierra Petrel, might occur as an accidental in the central North Pacific. It has a larger bill than Cook's, may have a more highly contrasting black patch behind the eye, has the white from the throat hooking up behind the eye, and, on the average, shows less white in the outer tail feathers. Each of these characters is subjective and each a hard call at sea.

Top: *Stejneger's Petrel (p. 60).* (*Gary Friedrichsen*) Bottom: *Cook's Petrel (p.58).* (*Peter Pyle*)

Stejneger's Petrel

(Pterodroma longirostris)

Probably an uncommon or rare straggler to the California Pacific, with only one record inside the 200-mile boundary. A single bird was well seen over very deep water between the Santa Lucia escarpment and the Davidson Seamount, about 80 miles west of Morro Bay, on 17 November 1979. Several Cook's Petrels were in the same area at the same time. Stejneger's Petrels nest on islands off the west coast of Chile, and at least some of the population moves north across the Equator toward Japan. Like so many *Pterodroma* petrels, Stejneger's at-sea distribution is poorly understood because of coverage and identification problems. Stejneger's may swing to the Eastern Pacific during their southbound migration in October and November. Like Cook's Petrel and Red-tailed Tropicbird, Stejneger's Petrel is likely a regular visitor to California waters beyond the distance capabilities of one-day pelagic trips.

Identification. In flight, Stejneger's appears to have unmarked white underwings, a trait it shares only with Cook's Petrel among *Pterodromas* in the North Pacific. Two white "checks" along the underwing border are a mark unique to Stejneger's. Also distinguishing it from Cook's are Stejneger's distinctly darker upperparts; this is especially notable in the blackish cap that includes the eye and sharply contrasts the white forecrown, lores, and cheek and the gray back. The black cap is especially dark, even "glossy" on fresh birds in November, when they seem to be most likely to appear in the nearshore Pacific. The white of a Stejneger's head hooks behind its eye unlike that in White-winged Petrel (not yet detected here). Because the dorsal wing surfaces are wholly darker than those of Cook's, the open W pattern across the extended wings, though present, is less obvious on Stejneger's. Cook's have white outer tail feathers (very hard to see). Stejneger's have dark ones.

Notes. The 1979 sight record remains the nearest reported from North American waters, but four individuals collected by Rollo H. Beck in mid-November 1906, "600 miles off San Francisco," and identified as *Pterodroma leucoptera* (White-winged Petrel) are, in fact, *P. longirostris* and are in the collection of the California Academy of Sciences. A check of coordinates on the original labels revealed that one was off San Francisco, one off Los Angeles, and two off Morro Bay: none was as far as

600 miles. Stejneger's, not White-winged, has definitely occurred off California. Five more were seen 200–300 miles off Southern California in mid-November 1989. Since all Eastern Pacific records fall in mid-November, that certainly seems the best time to look for Stejneger's. It, as well as Cook's, should be looked for well offshore.

Streaked Shearwater
(Calonectris leucomelas)

Extremely rare, in fall. This large, distinctive shearwater has been documented on only five occasions in the near-shore Pacific. All five individuals were seen from boats in Monterey Bay, and all records were between 22 September and 14 October of five different years between 1975 and 1985. An individual captured alive and released on 2 August 1989 at Laysan Island is the only other record for the Northeast Pacific.

Identification. This is a big shearwater, basically white below and gray-brown above, with a white face containing black streaks. The nape, back, and rump are gray-brown, as are the upperwing coverts, and pale feather *edges* cause these areas to appear scaly. Blackish flight feathers (the big feathers of the wing and all the tail feathers) contrast the slightly paler upperparts. The uppertail coverts are white, sometimes showing as a white "horseshoe" between the rump and tail but sometimes hidden from view. The underbody is white with varying amounts of brownish flecking onto the sides of the neck and chest. The underwings are mostly white, including the wingpits (axillaries), but the black flight feathers show as a broad trailing margin and wingtip. The ventral primary coverts are dark, causing a small triangular dark wedge in the otherwise white underwing just outside the wrist. The legs and feet are pink, as is the black-tipped bill.

No other bird species looks much like the unique Streaked Shearwater, but please remember that partially albinistic shear-waters do occur rarely. Aberrant Pink-footed or Buller's shear-waters with white faces have caused errors in identification.

Behavior. Flight is heavy and lumbering like that of Flesh-footed and Pink-footed shearwaters, but the wing is more often held angled at the wrist. Like other shearwaters, Streaked is gre-

Top left: *Pink-footed Shearwater (p. 63). (Rich Stallcup)* Top
right: *Streaked Shearwater (p. 61), showing underwing, behind
wing of a dark Wedge-tailed Shearwater. (Alan McBride)* Bottom:
Streaked Shearwater, dorsal view. (Alan McBride)

garious and may be attracted to chum served from boats. At least two of the California birds, though, were alone and very near the beach: whether this suggests they were not well or that these are traits of the species is not now known to us.

Notes. Streaked Shearwaters nest on islands off the coast of the Western Pacific, from the Soviet Union south to Japan, and some move south to the Equator (north of New Guinea) during the at-sea period.

Though unrecorded in Australia before 1979, Streakeds are now often found off the northern and northeastern shores of that continent. The apparent change there may indicate a true shift in the species' range. Here in the Eastern Pacific, the burst of records is more likely due to the recent enthusiastic coverage by field ornithologists, enabling them to detect strays that wandered to nearshore waters, probably along fingers of warm-water currents.

Pink-footed Shearwater
(Puffinus creatopus)

Common in fall (August through October) and rare from December through March, when numbers begin building again to the fall peak.

Identification. A big, relatively slow-flying, broad-winged, "white-bellied" shearwater that (except for very dark trailing edges to the wings and a contrasting dark tail) is *uniform* gray-brown above. The underparts are white, but the dark and light definition is blurred where the cheek meets the throat and in the wingpits. The underwings contain much white in the core but are broadly margined with black, bits of which intrude into the white. This is a variable trait: some individuals have darker underwings than others. Full sunlight on the underwings of a light individual (e.g., early morning sunlight on a wheeling bird) makes it look immaculate at a distance, and at such a time it might easily be mistaken for another species, like Buller's Shearwater. The bill of Pink-footed is always pink with a dark tip, and the legs and feet are pink. When inspecting a bird on the water, look for the gray-white throat and chest, pink-based bill, and uniform gray-brown upperparts.

Flesh-footed Shearwater, which is the same size and shape as

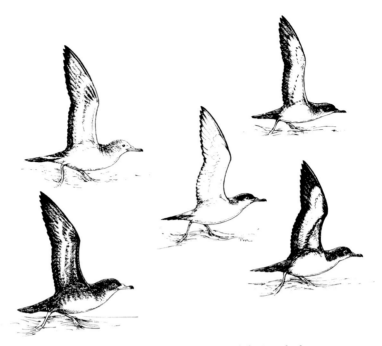

White-bellied shearwaters, ventral views. Top left: *Streaked Shearwater (p. 61).* Top right: *Black-vented Shearwater (p. 74).* Middle: *Buller's Shearwater (p. 69).* Lower left: *Pink-footed Shearwater (p. 63).* Lower right: *Wedge-tailed Shearwater (p. 68).* *(Tim Manolis)*

(and possibly just a dark form of) Pink-footed, also has a pink-based, dark-tipped bill but is all dark in plumage. Pink-footed's flight manner is very different from that of the swift and agile Buller's and Wedge-tailed shearwaters and from the faster, more twinkling gait of Black-vented and Townsend's. On the water, Pink-footeds sometimes show very little white (especially when facing away from the boat, as they usually do) and then may look much like Flesh-footeds.

Behavior. Flight is heavy and lumbering. The rather slow flapping is broken by some gliding and occasional wheeling on stiff wings, more frequent as the wind increases. Some individuals follow boats for chum, whereas others, full of food or just traveling, ignore them. Pink-footed may be solitary or gregarious but is seldom found in homogeneous flocks with its own kind.

Notes. This species nests on islands off Chile during winter in California, then moves mostly north along the coast. It is basically a citizen of the Eastern Pacific.

White-bellied shearwaters, dorsal views. Top left: *Streaked Shearwater (p. 61).* Top right: *Black-vented Shearwater (p.74).* Middle: *Buller's Shearwater (p. 69).* Lower left: *Pink-footed Shearwater (p. 63).* Lower right: *Wedge-tailed Shearwater (p. 68).* *(Tim Manolis)*

Flesh-footed Shearwater

(Puffinus carneipes)

Rather rare in fall and found where there are large numbers of other shearwaters. Very rare at other seasons, but records are scattered throughout the year. Though regular in fall, seldom more than one or two (if any) are seen per trip.

Identification. A big, relatively slow-flying, broad-winged, "dark-bellied" shearwater. Flesh-footed is very dark throughout its plumage, with shadowed underwings no lighter than the rest of the bird. When illuminated by direct, flat sunlight, the structure of the flight feathers results in reflection causing them to appear whiter than the dark coverts, much like those of Turkey Vulture. The large bill is pink or pinkish-horn at the base and black-tipped. The legs and feet are pink or pasty white, best seen as the bird is water-running to gain flight. On the water, scan dark-headed and dark-breasted shearwaters for this species' obviously clashing, light-colored bill.

The large size, distinctly dark underwings, and pale bill will separate this species from all but dark Wedge-tailed Shearwaters. Flesh-footed is heavier with broader wings, a much shorter tail, and also a very different flight style (see under Wedge-tailed Shearwater). Immature Heermann's Gulls, which sometimes associate with shearwaters, are similarly dark blackish-brown all over and have pink-based, black-tipped bills, but they are smaller, have black legs and feet, fly buoyantly, and are obviously gulls, not shearwaters. Heermann's are frequently mistaken for Flesh-footeds if the gull is sitting with shearwaters and the observer is, well, enthusiastic.

Behavior. Flight is heavy and lumbering. The rather slow flapping is broken by some gliding and occasional wheeling on stiff wings, more frequent as the wind increases. Flesh-footed Shearwater is often attracted to small boats for chum. The few individuals here are usually found associating with other species of shearwaters in mixed flocks.

Notes. Formerly known as Pale-footed Shearwater, this species is apparently very close, taxonomically and behaviorally, to Pink-footed Shearwater, and in the future the two might be found to be morphologically different races of the same species.

Greater Shearwater
(Puffinus gravis)

One individual was seen and very well described by highly experienced seabirders at Monterey Bay on 24 February 1979. Its placement on the California state list and its debut to the Pacific Ocean have been accepted by the California Bird Records Committee.

Identification. A large, long-winged shearwater with a black cap, white nape, scaly gray upperparts, white rump, and black tail. It is mostly white below, with underwings margined narrowly in black and a smudgy gray patch on the belly. In addition to other "white-bellied" shearwaters, large *Pterodroma* petrels (like Juan Fernandez) must be considered before concluding the identification of a bird so far out of range.

Notes. Because Greater Shearwater's occurrence in the Northeast Pacific was such a surprise, and because it may be a very

Top: *Flesh-footed Shearwater (p. 65). (Alan McBride)* Bottom left:
Greater Shearwater (p. 66), dorsal view. (Mike Danzenbaker)
Bottom right: *Greater Shearwater, ventral view. (Ed Harper)*

long time before it appears again, we won't write more about it here. It is a bird of the Atlantic, and the California individual no doubt slipped around Tierra del Fuego and proceeded north.

Wedge-tailed Shearwater
(Puffinus pacificus)

Rare, with only two records from California: one was a light-phase bird, seen four miles west of Point Piños, Monterey County, on 31 August 1986 (the first United States record); the other was a dark-phase bird at the north end of the Salton Sea, Riverside County, on 31 July 1988. This latter bird likely became trapped at the north end of the Gulf of California (as do many waterbirds in late summer) and flew overland. The species regularly occurs off the tip of Baja California, offshore western Mexico, and throughout the Eastern Tropical Pacific, so we might expect records to increase here in the future because of warming ocean waters.

Identification. This shearwater is most like Buller's in size, shape, and flight mannerisms, but its tail is half again as long, much wider, and more flamboyant. The body is thin and elongate. Wings are long and slim except near the body, where long secondaries make them wide. The upperparts are entirely dark brown, the only pattern being produced by pale tips to the greater wing coverts. These form one or two subtly lighter stripes at the base of the primaries and along the dorsal trailing edge of the wing near the base of the secondaries.

Dark-phase birds are all brown below as well as above, some with underwings almost as dark as in Flesh-footed Shearwater, others with a ghost of the pattern of light-phase birds. Light-phase birds are dark brown above, much like dark-phase ones. The chin, throat, breast, side, belly, and flanks are pure white, but their demarcation with the dark upperparts is rather blurred. The underwings are mostly white. The dark exceptions are the narrow leading and broad trailing edges of the underwing, the axillaries, and a diagonal line from just inside the wrist on the leading edge to the posterior axillaries (which isolates a small triangle of white on the forward base of the underwing). The tail and undertail coverts are dark. There are intermediate-phase birds.

The bill of all color phases is gray-based and black-tipped, sometimes appearing all black. Legs and feet are pasty pink, but the outer part of the outer web, the outer toe, and outer edge of the leg may be dark. It is said that white toenails are unique to this species (but this is really hard to see in the field).

Behavior. The flight is extremely graceful, like that of Buller's, with effortless flapping broken by sustained gliding on bowed wings. Flaps are smooth, unlike the more labored flaps of Pink-footed or Flesh-footed Shearwater, and Wedge-tailed uses lift from the waves more efficiently.

When competing for food, Wedge-taileds often fly with legs and feet hanging down, close their necks a bit (giving them an "Adam's apple" look), and blatantly use their large tails to out-maneuver even small gulls. They sometimes quarter their bodies to drop on floating food items, reminiscent of the behavior of a harrier.

Notes. Wedge-tailed Shearwater is widespread in the Equatorial Pacific (and Indian Ocean) but breeds as close to California as San Benedicto Island in the Revillagigedos off Mexico and in Hawaii, where the population is estimated at 1.5 million birds (85% light phase).

Buller's Shearwater
(Puffinus bulleri)

Normally occurs in California waters *only in the fall,* from late July through November, with a probable peak in late September. It is common most years in Northern California from Point Sur northward and decidedly uncommon from there south. There are a couple of winter records, each of a single individual.

Identification. A really striking bird that, because of its grace in movement, may not be done justice by an illustration or single-frame photograph. Buller's is immaculately white below, margined narrowly and crisply on the underside of the wings by black. Above, it is distinctly black-capped and gray-backed and shows an obvious black-on-gray extended M pattern on the dorsal wing surfaces. On the water Buller's shows more gleaming white than Pink-footed or Black-vented shearwaters, and its black cap is very distinct.

Buller's are so white below and have such fancy patterning above that, given a reasonable view, typical individuals are unmistakable. No other shearwater is as white below, especially on the underwings, or as contrasting above. Juan Fernandez Petrel (*Pterodroma externa*), a tropical Pacific species that ranges close to the California Pacific, is superficially similar, but it displays the typical large-headed and big-bodied look of a *Pterodroma* petrel. Worn Buller's lose much dorsal patterning, and leucistic individuals (white-headed) have been seen. Such birds have been mistaken for Streaked Shearwaters.

Behavior. Buller's are narrow-winged, long-bodied shearwaters with long tails. Their efficient use of lift from ocean swells enables them to glide on bowed wings for long periods without flapping. In breeze there is much rolling and arcing. The birds are very agile while competing for food with other shearwaters and even gulls. Homogeneous flocks are sometimes encountered, and their synchronized flight is beautifully graceful. Individuals or small groups often follow birders' boats to eat bits of chum.

Notes. Buller's Shearwater has occurred once inland, at the north end of the Salton Sea on 6 August 1966 (specimen), and once in the Atlantic — a bird well photographed (28 October 1984, 31 miles east-southeast of Baregat Light, New Jersey). Much like the Monterey Greater Shearwater, that bird probably rounded the tip of South America into the wrong ocean and moved north.

This species may sometimes be seen from shore. An exceptionally large concentration were the 7,200 that remained very near Point Reyes Lighthouse in late September and early October 1987. Flocks of more than 1,000 were seen from Southeast Farallon Island during the autumns of 1985, 1986, and 1987.

Buller's nest at Poor Knight's Island, northern New Zealand, from November through March, and cruise around the Eastern and Central Pacific the rest of the year.

Sooty Shearwater
(Puffinus griseus)

U sually the most abundant shearwater off California. During the late summer many, many hundreds of thousands migrate nearshore and may often be seen from land, causing even surfers and beachcombers to wonder what is going on. The species remains very common into early October, when numbers begin to decrease. It is uncommon to rare from December to late March (when Short-tailed Shearwaters are also present and at times outnumber Sooties). Numbers then begin to build again toward the massive passage in late summer.

Identification. A medium-sized shearwater that is all dark blackish-brown except for the underwing coverts, which are shining white and show as a blaze. The bill, legs, and feet are black. In summer, some individuals in heavy molt appear to have white wing stripes dorsally as well as ventrally.

The only similar species is Short-tailed Shearwater, and the two are *so* similar that even experienced seabirders will often argue the identity of a well-seen individual. For a discussion of the problem, see Short-tailed Shearwater. Symmetrically leucistic birds occur rarely and have been mistaken for other species, even the flashy Cape Petrel *(Daption capense)*.

Behavior. During normal flight, Sooty Shearwater's wing beats are more clipping than those of Flesh-footed, and it flies more directly with less soaring and gliding than does Wedge-tailed. As in all shearwaters, though, wheeling and stiff-winged gliding increase with the wind velocity. While a few individuals may be attracted to boats by chumming, most Sooty Shearwaters ignore them and pass by.

Short-tailed Shearwater
(Puffinus tenuirostris)

T he status of this species has changed in the last century in California waters. It was formerly considered common nearshore during much of the year, but recent records show that it is now decidedly uncommon, most frequent during winter.

Because of Short-tailed's strong similarity to Sooty Shearwater, the precise status and distribution of Short-tailed may be

Top left: *Wedge-tailed Shearwater (p. 68), dark phase, dorsal view. (Paul Crawford)* Top right: *Wedge-tailed Shearwater, light phase, ventral view. (Rich Stallcup)* Inset: *Buller's Shearwater (p. 69), dorsal view. (Stephen F. Bailey)* Middle: *Buller's Shearwater, ventral view. (Alan Hopkins)* Bottom: *Sooty Shearwater (p. 71). (Ed Harper)*

more finely detailed in the future. For now we may call it an uncommon winter visitor, with records from mid-September through April but only to be *expected* from early October through March. Though Short-tailed is highly gregarious where it is common, most observations here are of single individuals, sometimes loosely associating with Sooty or other shearwater species.

Identification. Slightly smaller than the *very* similar Sooty Shearwater, and caution must be used when identifying this much rarer bird. The best characteristics for separating the two, though slight, are Short-tailed's smaller, rounder head; its shorter, narrower bill; its narrower, more sticklike wings; and in some birds, a dark-capped/light-chinned look. Tail length is not a reliable field mark for identification.

Body color and underwing pattern, both formerly thought to be useful field marks, now seem practically worthless for many individual birds. Due to molt and normal variation, both species may show various amounts and distribution of white in the underwing and may at times look exactly alike in this regard. *Some* Sooties — with the classic blaze of silvery-white — and *some* Short-taileds — with uniform smoke-gray or brownish underwings — might be identified on those features alone, but many others cannot. In spring (March, April), Short-taileds are uniformly warm brown above and below and are easier to separate from the darker Sooties at this time. The two are so close, however, that many individuals will have to pass as unidentified. Just wish them well, and look for clearer examples.

Behavior. A medium-sized, dark-bellied shearwater with a much snappier wing beat than the lumbering gait of Flesh-footed or Pink-footed shearwater and a more frantic demeanor than the flowing grace of Buller's or Wedge-tailed.

A larger *percentage* of Short-taileds than Sooties seem to be attracted to boats chumming for birds, and a dark shearwater that flies right up the center of the wake and dives for tidbits behind the boat should be especially scrutinized. On many occasions we have seen an individual Short-tailed return to the boat (which, of course, is moving) four or five times over a period of perhaps five hours. We have yet to prove the much more common Sooty Shearwater doing this trick, though some become attracted briefly to food scraps in the wake.

Dark-bellied shearwaters. Top: three Short-tailed Shearwaters (p. 71), showing variations in plumage. Bottom left: Flesh-footed Shearwater (p. 65). Bottom right: Sooty Shearwater (p. 71). (Tim Manolis)

Black-vented Shearwater

(Puffinus opisthomelas)

When the nearshore, north-flowing Davidson Current is strong and warm, this species usually appears at least as far north as Point Reyes by late September, remaining into early December. In some years it may be considered common, with flocks seen that number into the hundreds and remain throughout the spring. Other years may find Black-vented Shearwaters mostly or wholly absent. Irregular incursions such as that in 1984 (when over 100 were present at Monterey as early as 22 August, 750 were estimated between Southeast Farallon Island and San Francisco on 10 October, and 5,000 + were carefully estimated on a pelagic trip at Monterey on 20 October) may become more routine with warming seas. In the early part of this century, Rollo Beck (1910) suggested this species' seasonal presence at Monterey from late July through late April. Periods of rarity or absence probably reflect cooler surface temperatures. Black-vented Shearwater becomes increasingly common farther south along the California coast and especially along the Pacific side of the Baja California peninsula. Reports are scarce for Northern California and northward, but they include specimens from Albert Head, British Columbia, on 24 October 1891, in November 1891, and in February 1895. Persistent seawatching from headlands during "good years" will find the Black-vented Shearwater present patchily.

Identification. Most like a small version of a Pink-footed Shearwater, the Black-vented is uniform gray-brown to blackish-brown above and mostly white below. Varying amounts of muddy feathering in the white cheeks, neck, sides, and undertail coverts make the dark-light line of demarcation unclear. The underwing coverts are mostly white, but a dark leading edge and dark flight feathers give the underwings a wide contrasting margin. The bill is black or dark gray, and the legs and feet are black.

A close relative of several other small shearwaters of the world (the Manx complex), this bird's taxonomic placement has long been uncertain. Until recently it was considered conspecific with Manx Shearwater.

Behavior. Very small (for shearwaters) and fast-flying, with clippy wing beats compared to more lumbering and soaring species, Black-venteds could be (and have been) mistaken for flying murres when the view is less than good. They favor nearshore waters and may be seen more often from shore than from ocean-going vessels. An early November individual at Cordell Bank, 25 miles west of Point Reyes Lighthouse, was exceptional.

Notes. Black-vented Shearwaters nest on islands off Baja California and, unlike most Pacific shearwater species, are not wide-ranging. Their preference for nearshore waters is demonstrated by their occurrence, as seen from birding trips, from Mission Bay (San Diego) to San Clemente Island, 80 miles to the west. Because the Black-vented's corridor is only 1 to 4 miles off the beach (and seldom farther offshore), the species is usually only seen in the first and last hour of these trips — when it's very nearly dark. Observers that miss these birds in the morning have one more chance — the same narrow band on the return trip, in late afternoon.

Top: *Short-tailed Shearwater (p. 71), a pale-throated, dark-capped individual. (Richard Webster)* Inset: *Townsend's Shearwater (p. 77). (Joseph R. Jehl, Jr.)* Middle left: *Black-vented Shearwater (p. 74), dorsal view. (Richard Webster)* Middle right: *Black-vented Shearwater, ventral view. (Mike Danzenbaker)* Bottom: *Townsend's Shearwater. (Joseph R. Jehl, Jr.)*

Townsend's Shearwater
(Puffinus auricularis)

Not yet officially accepted as having occurred in near-shore California waters, or anywhere else near North America north of Mexico, this species has been reported over deep water west of Cordell Bank, Marin County; it was well seen on 16 June 1985 by two highly experienced sea-bird observers familiar with the species from the Eastern Tropical Pacific. Perhaps we will see an increase of northward occurrences for Townsend's Shearwater, as well as Wedge-tailed and other semitropical species, as warming water trends continue.

Identification. Smaller even than Black-vented Shearwater but longer tailed, Townsend's is very dark brown to black above and sharply contrasting bright white below. The underwings are white-centered, with black margins front and rear that are mostly clear-cut. Except for the face, sides of the neck, drumsticks, tail, and undertail coverts — which are black — the rest of the underparts, including the axillaries, are white. Oval-shaped white patches (rather like those of Violet-green Swallow) extend from the lower flanks upward into the sides of the bird's black lower back; they may be the most easily seen and conclusive feature. The bill is long, thin, and black, and the legs and feet are pasty-white. On the water the bird's uniform blackish upperparts strikingly contrast with its white chin, throat, and foreneck.

No other shearwater in the nearshore Pacific is as uniform blackish above and white below. Only the Black-vented Shearwater is as small as Townsend's, but the former's brown upperparts, which "mud" into its whitish face, neck, breast, and underwings, and its short tail as well, should clearly distinguish the two. Audubon's Shearwater *(Puffinus lherminieri),* which *could* occur here, lacks the large black collar and white flank patch of Townsend's. A bird seen on 27 August 1977 in Monterey Bay matched Manx Shearwater *(Puffinus puffinus),* a cold-water Atlantic Ocean bird seen occasionally in the South Pacific, but "Newell's" (the Hawaiian race of Townsend's) could not be discounted. The fact that Manx types are occasionally seen in Alaskan waters lends support to the former choice. Newell's and the more eastern Pacific Townsend's are tropical birds that do not seem to range far from home.

Behavior. Wing beats are quick and choppy (even more so than those of the similar Black-vented), and, like most shearwaters, Townsend's flies near the water's surface without much gliding when the breeze is low. Also like most shearwaters, when the breeze comes up, so does the bird, and its set-wing soaring and arcing increase.

Notes. A thorough discussion, "The Biology and Taxonomy of Townsend's Shearwater," is presented by Jehl (1982).

Storm-Petrels. Family Hydrobatidae

Of 20 extant species in the world, 8 are documented as having occurred in the nearshore Pacific; 4 of these nest on offshore islands here.

Though small and dainty-looking when compared to other tubenoses, storm-petrels are just as thoroughly at home on the open sea and are able to survive monsoons and hurricanes. Mexican mariners call the storm-petrel *la golondrina de la tempestad* or "swallow of the storm."

The flight behavior of storm-petrels as a group is unique, but subtle differences between species are often diagnostic. Their basic flight style is a series of deep, staccato wing strokes interspaced with short glides. Some species' wing strokes are more deep and cleaving than others? Some birds zig-zag, others rollercoaster. Some fly on-line, whereas others perform quick arcs on set wings. Most species flutter and pitter-pat their feet on the water surface (like Saint Peter, from which the word *petrel*), some so often that this is a prominent behavior.

Storm-petrels are mostly black, black and white, or gray. Like many true ocean birds, they do much or all of their foraging at night, when small pelagic organisms percolate to the surface.

Wilson's Storm-Petrel
(Oceanites oceanicus)

Rare in fall. Almost every year 1 to 5 are found within the great storm-petrel flocks on Monterey Bay from August to November. Since 10,000 birds may be scattered in small flocks over a square mile of water, and since they are very spooky and trade places a lot, it is hard to pin down exact numbers, even small ones. Over the years at Monterey, there are about 30 fall records of Wilson's Storm-Petrel, but since these birds are long-lived it is very likely that many of those records are returns by the same individuals. One there on 1 May 1978 and 1 off Point Reyes in June 1989 are the only spring records. Up until 1985 there were only about 5 records for the rest of California. On 3 and 5 November 1985, an astounding assemblage of procellarids at Cordell Bank yielded 45 Wilson's Storm-Petrels, more than the previous combined totals for the entire North Pacific. On 13 August 1989, 10 were present at Cordell Bank. The nearshore distribution and status of this species clearly remain a mystery.

Identification. A medium-sized, white-rumped storm-petrel that is quite black except for obvious tan carpal bars. The saddle-shaped white rump extends down to the lateral undertail coverts (as in Band-rumped) and can be seen at most angles, even when the bird is sitting. The wings are more rounded than those of our other storm-petrel species, giving them a special look in flight. The tail, too, is rounded (other white-rumped species have notched or forked tails) and can often be seen because of the bird's special behaviors (see below.) The legs are long, so the yellow webs extend beyond the tip of the tail in flight. The webs may be seen more easily if the bird is close and dancing on the water.

Behavior. Flight is direct, with low, fluttering, butterfly-like strokes, and it does not involve bouncing side to side (like Leach's) or up and down (like Band-rumped). Fluttering flight is occasionally interrupted by steep upswoops, sometimes in combination with shrug preening, and during these behaviors the unique tail shape can often be seen. When foraging, Wilson's just seem to dangle like little marionettes, on open wings, pattering on the surface with their long legs much extended. This pattering behavior is frequent for Wilson's, occasional for Band-rumped, and seldom for Leach's.

Top and middle: *Wilson's Storm Petrel (p. 78). (Mike Danzenbaker)*
Bottom: *Least Storm-Petrel (p. 81). (Bernie Tershy and Craig Strong)*

Least Storm-Petrel
(Oceanodroma microsoma)

Irregular in late summer; sometimes abundant off Southern California; and, although not recorded each year at Monterey, has appeared there in good numbers (possibly up to 1,000 in October 1983). Least Storm-Petrel has been recorded as far north as Humboldt County, California (once, on 1 October 1972). It is much more likely to be found in the California Pacific during periods of warm water. In years when the species is scarce or absent off Southern California, reports from Northern California are probably in error.

Identification. The smallest storm-petrel, Least is all dark blackish, like Black Storm-Petrel and unlike the brown Ashy Storm Petrel. It has a wedge-shaped tail that looks relatively short and gives the species a batlike look. Its flight is fairly direct, with deep and high wing beats similar to those of the Black Storm-Petrel but more rapid.

Black, Ashy, and dark-rumped Leach's storm-petrels are all larger and slower, with longer tails. While the flight of Black is similar to Least's, it is slower. In at-ease flight, Ashies lack the high wing stroke of Least (or Leach's or Black) and have a more rowing gait. Leach's bounce around the waves, side to side and up and down (compared to Least's more direct flight), but they too have a high wing stroke.

Behavior. A nearshore species, Least is gregarious at sea and is often found sitting in tight flocks with Black or Ashy storm-petrels. Though lone individuals are sometimes seen, they are most often in an area of scattered birds searching for food or represent fragments of a roosting flock disturbed earlier.

Notes. In early September 1976, Hurricane Kathleen lifted 500 to 1,000 Least Storm-Petrels from the Sea of Cortez and deposited them at the Salton Sea in the Southern California desert and along the Colorado River between California and Arizona. A few apparently healthy birds remained into late October. No corpses were found, suggesting that possibly the birds made it back to kinder waters.

The Least nests on islands on both sides of the Baja California peninsula, where some birds are resident while others disperse south to northern South America.

Wedge-rumped Storm-Petrel
(Oceanodroma tethys)

Very rare nearshore. There are fewer than 15 records for the California Pacific. Nine of these are from well off-shore Southern California, and 3 are from the vicinity of Monterey Bay. The first was captured in the village of Carmel on 21 January 1969 after five days of southerly gales. The specimen proved to be of the southern, Peruvian race *(O. t. kelsalli)*, the first North American record for the subspecies and the first United States record for the species. Another, a healthy bird, was studied with big flocks of other storm-petrel species on Monterey Bay on 24 September and 1 October 1977, and a third was flying southwest near Point Piños on 2 October 1984.

Identification. This bird is small, like Least Storm-Petrel, but has a longer tail mostly covered above by the exceptionally long white uppertail coverts, which narrow dorsally toward the tail tip, forming a white triangle. Wedge-rumped's flight, too, is like that of Least, with high wing strokes, and the motion is fairly direct but perhaps a bit more erratic and three-dimensional.

Wedge-rumped is told from other white-rumped species by its small size and its flight behavior, as well as the unique tail-covert pattern, all of which are diagnostic. Whereas other species (like Wilson's) usually show white lower flanks when sitting, Wedge-rumpeds usually do not.

Behavior. Like other storm-petrels, Wedge-rumped is usually gregarious with its own or other storm-petrel species. Its flight is more direct than that of Leach's or Band-rumped. The high wing elevation before each downstroke is unlike that of Ashy, Fork-tailed, or Wilson's.

Notes. Formerly known as Galapagos Storm-Petrel.

Band-rumped Storm-Petrel
(Oceanodroma castro)

Very rare and local. A single individual was observed at close range for a long time period near San Clemente Island, west of San Diego, on 12 September 1970. This was the only record for California (and for the west coast of North America) until nine Band-rumped Storm-Petrels were identified on 20 July 1989 in California waters, 120 to 160 miles southwest of San Nicolas Island (Peter Pyle), and another was seen nearer the island one week later (*fide* Dick Veit). It is likely that some Pacific Band-rumped Storm-Petrels disperse north to certain warm-water areas during late summer, as this species does in the Atlantic off North Carolina. They would likely be found in the same waters frequented by Cook's Petrels, especially along a convergence area variably 100 to 200 miles south-southwest of San Nicolas Island.

Identification. A large storm-petrel, all blackish except for tan carpal bars and a bright white rump that sharply curls down onto the lateral undertail coverts. For most storm-petrels, flight mannerisms will be the best clue to specific identification. Band-rumped's flight is rather like that of Leach's, but it moves *on-line* — straight during calm or with much bouncing up and down like a Ping-Pong ball in high winds — with less of the side-to-side zigging and zagging so typical of Leach's Storm-Petrel. Its acrobatics are occasionally interrupted by stiff-winged, Spotted Sandpiper–like flap-gliding.

Leach's Storm-Petrel is certainly the most similar species, but also consider Wilson's and Wedge-rumped. From Leach's, the Band-rumped differs in its shorter, less forked tail, its shorter wings with a less obvious carpal bar (variable, dependent upon wear), and its gleaming but narrow white rump, which is extensive and includes the lateral tail coverts and even some crissal feathers. Its flight is less erratic than that of Leach's, and its glides and stiff-winged flapping may be unique. Its legs are shorter than those of Wilson's Storm-Petrel, and, unlike Wilson's, the toes do not extend beyond the end of the tail. Band-rumpeds are clearly larger than Wedge-rumpeds, and their flight and plumage are very different.

Behavior. Except for flight characteristics, Band-rumped is much like other storm-petrels in behavior, but perhaps more inclined to follow boats that are chumming or spilling food bits. The San Diego bird stayed near the boat for a long while, even coursing underneath extended fishing lines. Others have been observed to ignore boats. When feeding, Band-rumpeds do more surface pattering than Leach's but not as much as Wilson's.

Notes. Formerly known here as Harcort's Storm-Petrel and currently known also as Madeiran Storm-Petrel.

Top left and right: *Wedge-rumped Storm-Petrels (p. 82). (Peter Pyle)* Middle: *Leach's Storm-Petrel (p. 85). (Peter Pyle)* Bottom left and right: *Black Storm-Petrels (p. 86). (Bernie Tershy, Craig Strong, and Dawn Breese)*

Leach's Storm-Petrel

(Oceanodroma leucorhoa)

Fairly common in late summer in Southern California but rarely encountered nearshore in Northern California, even off Humboldt and Del Norte counties, where more than 15,000 Leach's nest on the rocks. Because of their pelagic nature and exclusively nocturnal travels to and from nests, the species is seldom seen at sea near that coast but is common year-round in outer waters. The few recent records off Monterey Bay are well beyond the continental shelf or are of birds blown to shore by northwest gales. Leach's do not roost with the large autumn flocks of Ashies and Blacks inside Monterey Bay, indicating their preference for deeper water farther offshore. The Farallon Islands host a breeding population of an estimated 1,400 pairs, and a scattered few birds probably nest in the Channel Islands. All of the California nesters are white-rumped, but dark-rumped birds disperse regularly into outer Southern California waters, especially in summer. A dark-rumped Leach's was found in Southern California's interior, at the Salton Sea, on 15 September 1976 following Hurricane Kathleen (see Least Storm-Petrel) and there are a couple of other inland records for the species.

Identification. The most variable and taxonomically perplexing North Pacific storm-petrel. Some (far northern) birds show nearly clear white rumps, whereas others (from Mexico) show rumps dark like the rest of the body. Though white-rumped birds are vastly more common in the California Pacific, dark-rumped birds occur in small numbers from far west of San Diego north, at least to waters west of the northern Channel Islands. Birds from Guadalupe Island are smaller and darker with brighter white rumps than other tropical Leach's.

Leach's is almost as large as Black Storm-Petrel but has a white rump. The white is partially divided by a dark bar and so appears as a double U that is *variously* smudgy, usually not bright white as in Wilson's Storm-Petrel. Leach's is told from other white-rumped species by the dark intrusions into the white rump. Band-rumped is the closest look-alike but is usually darker with a shorter, notched (not forked) tail, shorter, broader wings, and more rectangular, less oval-shaped white on the rump. Both Wilson's and Band-rumped have white extending prominently to the undertail area, a feature that Leach's rarely shows. Leach's flight is erratic and three-dimensional as it bounds up and down and side to side over and between the waves. Told from dark-rumped storm-petrels by size and distinctive ricocheting manner of flight. The flight mannerisms are diagnostic, and with experience, one can identify Leach's, even from Band-rumped, at a great distance.

Behavior. Less gregarious and more interested in deep ocean than our three dark-rumped storm-petrels, except over the warmer, more docile waters of extreme Southern California, where it is routinely found only a few miles west of the beach. These southern birds most likely are from island populations off Mexico and may have different needs and preferences than more northern birds, or perhaps those waters harbor edible organisms that colder ones do not.

Black Storm-Petrel

(Oceanodroma melania)

A common summer and fall visitor off Southern California and north to Monterey Bay. The species is rare in the Gulf of the Farallones and at Cordell Bank and has not been recorded north of Sonoma County. At Monterey, its numbers fluctuate as the result of water temperature trends. Its distribution is very similar to Least Storm-Petrel's; it nests on islands on both sides of the Baja peninsula, and most of the population disperses southward. Blacks have a small breeding outpost in U.S. waters with about 150 birds nesting on Sutil Rock near Santa Barbara Island.

Identification. Large and black (clearly darker than Ashy Storm-Petrel, which is brown) with tan carpal bars and a rather long, notched tail. The flight of Black Storm-Petrel is deliberate, and its wing beats are deep and *spaced*, reminiscent of the flight of a Black Tern. Like Least but unlike Ashy Storm-Petrel, it raises its wings definitely above horizontal before each downstroke. (Ashies only high-stroke when accelerating to gain flight.) Blacks do not fly in the bouncy, zig-zag manner that is typical of Leach's, and this is the best first clue for separating the two species. (Remember, there are dark-rumped Leach's from waters to the south.)

Behavior. Black Storm-Petrels are gregarious when at rest, often rafting with Leasts and Ashies, but in places where large numbers congregate, the species are often partitioned in homo-

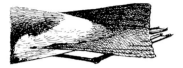

Typical rump-tail patterns for eight Pacific storm-petrels. Top to bottom, left: Least (p. 81), Ashy (p. 88), Black (p. 86), Fork-tailed (p. 91); right: Wilson's (p. 78), Wedge-rumped (p. 82), Band-rumped (p. 82), Leach's (p. 85). *(Keith Hansen)*

geneous groups, making ratios among them hard to determine. At Monterey, for example, one flock of 500 birds may be 90% Blacks and the next one 90% Ashies. Like other storm-petrels, Blacks are not usually interested in boats, even those baiting for birds, unless they make a special effort to spread a slick of shark-liver oil or similar animal fluids.

Notes. Black is the most frequent storm-petrel off Southern California, and individuals may sometimes be seen from shore there through telescopes.

Ashy Storm-Petrel
(Oceanodroma homochroa)

Common within the great storm-petrel flocks at Monterey Bay in fall and unpredictable elsewhere. Ashy is sometimes fairly common in summer in Southern California, from Santa Catalina Island north, and is sometimes found in numbers in the Gulf of the Farallones or at Cordell Bank in summer and fall. Elsewhere, singles or small groups may be found anywhere off California (and virtually nowhere else), but with

Observing storm-petrels from a boat. (Rich Stallcup)

Storm-petrel flock on Monterey Bay. The three foreground birds (not in scale to one another) are, left to right, Black (p. 86), Ashy (p.88), and Least (p. 81). (Keith Hansen)

the bulk of Ashy's world population concentrated in Monterey Bay, there aren't many more birds to go around. Its winter range is poorly known, as most Ashies depart nearshore California at that time.

Except for a wee few Ashy Storm-Petrels reported from Los Coronados Islands off Tijuana, Baja California, the whole world population nests on islands and islets off California — over 75% (an estimated 4,000 birds) on the Farallones and most of the rest on San Miguel, Santa Cruz, and Santa Barbara in the Channel Islands.

Identification. A medium-sized storm-petrel, the Ashy is all brown with lighter wing linings (unique) and a long tail that in profile appears sometimes to curl up a bit at the end. During at-ease flight, Ashy's wing beat rhythm is intermediate between the Black's and the Least's but is shallower than either of the others'. Before the downstroke, Ashy raises its wings only to the horizontal, not high above it (as Black and Least do). Flight is on-

Ashy Storm-Petrels (p. 88). Top: *dorsal view. (Richard Webster)*
Bottom: *flock. (Rich Stallcup)*

line. No matter their typical flight style, all these species fly with high strokes when accelerating from the water to take off.

Ashies are browner than Blacks or Leasts and even sometimes appear to have a grayish cast, but even in worn plumage they do not have the pale gray feathering present in Fork-tailed Storm-Petrel. The latter would match Ashy in flight silhouette more closely than the others.

Behavior. Like other storm-petrel species, Ashies are gregarious, and in this region are seldom found alone. Thousands (4,000–6,000) congregate at day roosts 3 to 12 miles off Moss Landing, along the north or south rims of the Monterey submarine canyon. This convention takes place throughout the autumn, with highest numbers present from September through mid-October. Often there are thousands of Black Storm-Petrels here, too, as well as scattered individuals of rare species.

Notes. A very large percentage (90%?) of the world's population of Ashy Storm-Petrels congregate in dense flocks on Monterey Bay in fall. At times they may all be on a single square mile of sea surface. While this is a spectacular wildlife spectacle, it is also very scary, as even a small oil spill at Moss Landing (certainly a possible event) could all but terminate the species.

Fork-tailed Storm-Petrel
(Oceanodroma furcata)

Now uncommon but might be found at any season; more often found north than south of Point Conception. Unlike most other storm-petrels, Fork-taileds prefer cold-water conditions. They breed from northernmost California north. Their distribution and seasonality are complicated. For the past 25 years this species has scarcely been found on boat trips off California, and most sightings have been of birds storm-blown to beaches and headlands or during "wrecks," the result of poor food winters such as 1976–1977 and 1989–1990. Even at the great storm-petrel roost on Monterey Bay, the Fork-tailed has rarely been present. Previously, though, during the 1950s and early 1960s (in years of generally cooler water), Fork-tailed Storm-Petrels were considered routine sightings in fall and winter from boats at Monterey and even on windless days were often the first true seabirds to be seen. We might expect the abundance status to change again from time to time.

Fork-tailed Storm-Petrels (p.91). Top: *dorsal view.(Peter LaTourette)* Bottom: *ventral view. (Rich Stallcup)*

Curiously, the species is regular in small numbers around Cordell Bank and west of the Farallones in *May and June*. Might a pair or two nest on some northern rock in the Farallon archipelago? A bird caught on Southeast Farallon in May 1990 clearly had an incubation patch and strengthens this suspicion.

Identification. This is the only light gray North Pacific storm-petrel, but phalaropes (especially Red) and other single shorebirds at sea have been mistaken for it. Storm-petrels have a buoyant, pumping flight (not hurried and frantic like the shorebirds'), and they appear relatively large-headed and long-tailed. The Fork-tailed is darker gray above than below, with a black rectangle (formed by several tracks of covert feathers) contrasting with the rest of its whitish underwing. Dark feathering is also present around its eye. In poor light, Ashy Storm-Petrels (which are about the same size and have similar flight mannerisms) may look pallid and are sometimes called Fork-taileds. This trick seldom works, though, as there is usually someone standing nearby who has been through the charade before — or else the bird flies into good light and quickly "molts" into a uniform *brown* plumage!

Behavior. Flight behavior of Fork-tailed Storm-Petrel is much like that of Ashy — being direct and on-line with fairly low, rowing strokes (unlike the higher, *cleaving* strokes of Black, Leach's, Least, and others). Fork-tailed is not as gregarious as some other species, but when present it often loosely associates with others of its kind.

Notes. About 300 pairs nest on rocks off Humboldt and Del Norte counties, and Fork-taileds become more and more numerous northward to the Aleutians and in the Gulf of Alaska. They also occur on the Asian side, off the Komandorskiye and Kurile islands, near the Kamchatcka Peninsula, and in the Sea of Okhotsk.

Top and inset: *Red-billed Tropicbirds (p. 95). (Ed Harper, top; Dawn Breese and Bernie Tershy, inset)* Bottom: *Red-tailed Tropicbird (p. 96). (Jack Swenson)*

Tropicbirds. Family Phaethontidae

Worldwide, there are three currently recognized tropicbird species, each of which has at least made its debut to the near-shore Pacific. Similar in size to medium or large gulls, their shape is narrower. With their mostly white plumage, colorful bills, and long central tail streamers, tropicbirds are spectacular.

Their normal flight is high above the sea and composed of nearly constant, rather deep wing beats, reminiscent of an accelerating falcon's. Unlike most ocean birds, tropicbirds seem to have only one gear — high, and full throttle. While in tropical tropicbird habitat, the wise seagoing naturalist looks straight up occasionally. Usually there is nothing there, but when the tropicbird appears, it makes all those other times seem worthwhile. When found away from nesting areas, tropicbirds are usually solitary.

Tropicbirds eat fish caught as the result of high-altitude plunge-dives. They normally have no interest in boats and, if seen at all, are often rapidly blending into distant clouds. Others may be seen riding buoyantly on the water, their tail streamers held aloft.

Courtship flights, unlikely to be witnessed here except perhaps at model glider airplane fields (see White-tailed Tropicbird account) are outrageous displays of precision flying and tandem, aerial break-dancing.

Red-billed Tropicbird
(Phaethon aethereus)

Rare in summer and fall off Southern California and accidental off the central portion of the state. Most records are from near the southern Channel Islands or west of them; there are virtually no records adjacent to the mainland. These are truly tropical seabirds. It is likely that more will be found when we begin to thoroughly survey the corridor from 50 to 100 miles offshore, especially at warm-water localities.

For the past six years, records have dwindled around the south end of San Clemente Island, where, historically, most state records have occurred. More recently, however, voyages have located a possible concentration area 50 to 60 miles west of the island. There are three records within 20 miles of the coast of Monterey County, two in July and one in October. Exceptional was a bird caught by fishermen on 18 June 1941 off Grays Harbor, Washington.

Identification. Unlike other tropicbirds, the Red-billed has primary feathers that are extensively black. Adults have red bills and white tail-streamers and are extensively barred with black on the nape, back, and rump. Immatures have narrow black nuchal bands from eye to eye and black-tipped tails.

Red-tailed and White-tailed tropicbirds are similar. Royal Terns near the Channel Islands are sometimes mistaken for tropicbirds, but this is more often a case of enthusiasm on the part of the observer rather than any true similarity.

Behavior. See family description, above. Good views of tropicbirds are usually had after one is spotted sitting on the water, because in flight they usually seem to be late for some distant appointment away from the boat and are anxious to keep it. They are usually high fliers.

Notes. Hurricane Kathleen knocked an immature to Morongo Valley, Riverside County, on 11 September 1976. It was then caught by a dog.

Red-tailed Tropicbird
(Phaethon rubricauda)

Accidental in the California Pacific, with the nearest nesting localities in the Hawaiian Islands, and perhaps the Revillagigedos, off Baja California. There are five records, four of which are in September and October between 100 and 200 miles west of different spots on the coast of Southern California. The only bird close to shore was an adult that circled the Southeast Farallon lighthouse on 3 July 1979. There are a few more records well seaward from the west coast of Baja California. This is another of the many warm-water species that will become a regular part of our nearshore avifauna once we are able to aggressively census deep water, the last North American ornithological frontier.

Identification. A large, broad-winged, heavy-flying tropic-bird, one that appears snow white. At any age there is virtually no black in the wings, especially from below. This feature alone should identify the species, but identification should be locked down by the red bill and red tail-streamers (the tail streamers often look white, except in perfect light). Immatures have all-white tails and, compared to juvenile Red-billeds, lack the black nuchal collar.

Behavior. See Red-billed Tropicbird; behavior is much the same in all three tropicbird species. Proportions and flight characteristics of Red-tailed are heavier than those of the other two and may remind one of a Cattle Egret.

Notes. Because this species has a broader distribution in the North Pacific than the others, it may turn out to be the most regular, well offshore here.

White-tailed Tropicbird
(Phaethon lepturus)

Accidental. There is only one record for the California Pacific. The nearest nesting area is in Hawaii. The one record was of a beautiful, full-tailed adult seen frequently between 24 May and 23 June 1964 from a bluff above Upper Newport Bay, the juiciest segment of Orange County, California. The bird was physically attracted to remote-controlled model glider airplanes, with which it sometimes flew in tandem. It was also noted trying to copulate with a yellow plane on the ground. It seemed to appear out of nowhere (as tropicbirds usually do) and upon departure would fly directly out to sea. The only other nearby record is of a bird found dead at Scottsdale, Arizona, following Hurricane Allen. Some were seen 300 to 500 miles off Southern California in early December 1989. Both of the onshore records have been assigned to the greenish-billed Pacific race, which is no surprise.

Identification. Smaller and daintier than the other two tropic-bird species. The upperparts are mostly white (no black barring), with black leading edges to the outer four or five primaries and a striking black bar across the innerwing. There is less black in the wingtips than in Red-billeds and more than in Red-taileds. Pacific birds tend to have greenish-yellow bills, and this feature alone would practically identify the species. Immature-plumaged

Top and inset: *White-tailed Tropicbirds (p. 97). (Jack Swenson)*
Bottom left and right: *Blue-footed Boobies (p. 100). (Peter Pyle, left; Ron LeValley, right)*

birds are seldom seen away from nest islands.

Behavior. Although most Americans who have seen White-tailed Tropicbirds may remember them in tandem flight zooming inside the crumbling walls of Old Fort Jefferson in the Dry Tortugas, diving headlong into volcanoes on Hawaii, or down cliffs on Kauai, their behavior at sea is quite different. See Red-billed Tropicbird, as behavior is much the same in all three tropicbird species.

Notes. The species is pantropical, with most birds clinging to warm-water zones.

Boobies. Family Sulidae

Of nine species in the world, four have appeared in the near-shore Pacific; none is regular. Closely related to pelicans but smaller, boobies' flight is similar, with decisive, pulsing wing beats interrupted by prolonged glides on bowed wings. Boobies also occasionally arc and rock in flight in a style reminiscent of large shearwaters. The wings are long and narrow, and the bird itself is long. Boobies in flight appear equally pointed at head, tail, and both wingtips (the head is located on the end showing forward progression). The large feet are totipalmate, like those of pelicans, with inclusive webbing of all four toes unique to the family. Boobies accomplish most feeding by plunge-diving on surface fish.

Tropical by nature, boobies become abundant not far south of Southern California and especially in the Sea of Cortez. From there, Brown and Blue-footed boobies make irregular visits in late summer to the Salton Sea in Imperial and Riverside counties.

These birds are well known as hitchhikers on the masts and rigging of ships, where they sit around looking like a bunch of boobies. Some or most extralimital records are probably of ship-assisted individuals.

Blue-footed Booby
(Sula nebouxii)

Very rare in the California Pacific. Most records for the coast and offshore zone have occurred following "invasions" from the northern Sea of Cortez to the Salton Sea. It is likely that many of the birds moving north continue from the Salton Sea westward through the desert at San Gorgonio Pass, and across Los Angeles to the Pacific. The most notable incursion (the largest flight to the Salton Sea) occurred in the fall of 1971, when about 35 individuals were recorded from coastal Southern California, and three individuals made it north to Lover's Point, Pacific Grove, Monterey County, on 16 October. Other coastal California records are an immature at Seal Rock, San Francisco, on 1 September 1977 and an adult at Point Saint George on 16 January 1981. There is one record north of California. A specimen was secured on 23 September 1935 near Everett, Washington.

Identification. All ages are white on the chest, belly, flanks, and undertail coverts, have a large white patch on the upper back, and have white rumps. All also have uniform dark grayish-brown dorsal wing surfaces and gray bills. Immatures have gray legs and feet that become bright blue as the birds age. Adults have white heads and necks, densely streaked with gray, whereas immatures' heads are more uniform light brown. The immature Masked Booby is the main look-alike, but its yellowish bill, dark hood, and white-striped inner dorsal wing coverts should be distinctive. It is good to remember that adult male Brown Boobies of the Eastern Pacific have frosty grayish heads and necks that, at a distance, resemble those of adult Blue-footed Boobies.

Behavior. Like Brown Boobies, Blue-footeds like to forage in clear shallow waters near the coast. Like other boobies, they fly high above the water and plunge-dive on fish near the surface. Blue-footeds, when found feeding, are often in groups. Whether this is a social event or an aggregation at abundant food, or both, is unknown. These birds will follow, and ride on, large vessels that are chumming or dumping organic garbage, and where the species is common, they can sometimes be hand-fed from small boats in calm waters. Boobies have not learned to fear humans and, when found on the ground, may usually be very closely approached.

Masked Booby

(Sula dactylatra)

Accidental in the California Pacific. A subadult individual was seen on 10 January 1977 at Cortez Bank about 25 miles south of San Clemente Island (the southernmost Channel Island), just north of the Mexican border, and an adult was seen flying over San Elijo Lagoon, San Diego County, on 14 November 1987. An immature was photographed from a fishing boat by skipper David Lemon 2 miles off Point Lobos, Monterey County, on 5 April 1990, and another, a juvenile, was photographed on 28 April 1988 at Isla Coronado Sur, 4 miles south of the United States–Mexico border. A common bird of the Eastern Tropical Pacific, with the nearest breeding colony (of about 50 pairs) at Alijos Rocks, 185 nautical miles (213 land miles) west of Cabo San Lazaro, which is about three-quarters of the way down the Baja peninsula. For a wide-ranging seabird with populations close to California, the near absence of records comes as a surprise. Perhaps if ocean temperatures continue in a warming trend, and we take more trips farther offshore from Southern California (maybe even in winter), the known status of Masked Booby will change. This species and Red-footed are far more pelagic than Brown and Blue-footed. Masked Booby was formerly called Blue-faced Booby.

Identification. Adults are unmistakable, with white bodies; black tails, primaries, secondaries, and facial feathers; and yellow bills, legs, and feet. Immatures have varyingly yellow bills, white breasts and bellies, and brownish hoods. Their upperparts are dark brown with white patches on the back, tail, and edges to the upperwing coverts forming white stripes. Some young birds have a complete white collar, but in most the hindneck is brown, connecting the brown back and hood.

Adults look like Gannets, but there are no Gannets in the North Pacific. Immatures are more tricky, looking rather like the Brown Booby below and the Blue-footed Booby above.

Behavior. When foraging, Masked Booby flies high above the sea, vertically plunge-diving into the water with partly open wings, often in pursuit of flying fish. Like Red-footeds, Masked Boobies are more pelagic than Brown and Blue-footed boobies, which are usually within a couple of miles of land.

Top: *Masked Booby (p. 101), adult. (Jack Swenson)* Inset: *Masked Booby, immature. (Dawn Breese and Bernie Tershy)* Bottom left: *Red-footed Booby (p. 103), white phase. (Jack Swenson)* Bottom right: *Red-footed Booby, brown phase. (Ron LeValley)*

Red-footed Booby
(Sula sula)

Rare in the California Pacific, but there are about eight nearshore records, including both white and brown phases. Two are from the Farallones: a dark-tailed bird on 12 August 1975, which after capture was measured and determined as *S. s. websterii*, the Mexican race; and a white-tailed bird seen on 12 October 1975, which may have been *S. s. rubripes* (from Hawaii). In Southern California, one adult (white phase) was seen to land on Morro Rock at Morro Bay, San Luis Obispo County, on 27 May 1985. One immature (brown phase) was recorded near Santa Barbara Island on 11 October 1987, and one immature (brown phase) off the north end of Santa Catalina Island on 15 November 1987. In Northern California, one associating with a small fishing fleet off northern San Mateo County 14 to 20 August 1987 roosted on Point San Pedro. Later the same year in September and October, a different Red-footed Booby adopted a group of boats fishing near the southern Marin County coast and for several days would ride the railing of the *Salty Lady* into the Golden Gate channel and around to Sausalito. It became droopy and was captured (with ease) for rehabilitation. It is still rehabilitating. On 8 October 1987, another landed on the A-frame of the Moss Landing Marine Lab's research vessel *Point Sur* about 12 miles west of Moss Landing and rode back to harbor, soon flying back to sea.

Unlike those of the other three North Pacific boobies, the nearest nesting localities for Red-footed are very far away, at Isla Revillagigedo, 400 miles south-southwest of Los Cabos, Baja Sur, and at Hawaii. Ship-assisted travel to California is likely involved in one or more of the species' California occurrences.

Identification. The smallest booby, with white- and dark-tailed races and each race containing both white- and dark-phased individuals. Except for leg, foot, and bill color, adult white-phase Red-footeds resemble adult Masked Boobies, but the former have white inner secondaries (not black), and in some individuals the tail is white. Dark-phase adults are mostly uniform medium-brown, as are immatures. The small size, blue bill, and red feet should identify the species.

Behavior. Like other boobies, but all California individuals have been either flying near or sitting on boats or on rocks.

Brown Booby
(Sula leucogaster)

Very rare in the California Pacific, with but few records, including two from Santa Barbara Island. A single bird summered at Prince Islet off San Miguel Island from 1961 to 1968; singles visited the Farallones on 24 April 1983 and 1 July 1984, and there are three records north on the coast as far as Monterey. Curiously, at the Salton Sea in the interior of Southern California, the Brown Booby is considered a "casual late summer visitor." Postbreeding dispersal sends birds to the northern end of the Gulf of California, then on across a narrow stretch of desert to the Salton Sea. There are many records, especially during the late 1960s and the 1970s. The Salton Sea is much more saline than the ocean, and many boobies "trapped" there perish, their nostrils often encrusted with salt.

Identification. Uniform brown above and hooded, with the dark brown hood sharply contrasting the white underparts and wing linings on adults and blending more with the paler brown underparts and wing linings of immatures. Adult males of the Eastern Pacific race *(S. l. brewsteri)* are smaller than females, and their heads are extensively frosted with pale gray. The bills of adults are yellow to dull green; those of younger birds are blackish to pale gray.

Behavior. Like other boobies, the Brown flies high when searching for food, plunge-diving vertically into the water to catch fish or squid. Individuals can be "chummed" to boats by tossed food, and they have even been hand-fed from launches off West Mexico. When perched, these, like other boobies, can usually be approached quite closely. A nearshore species (less pelagic than Red-footed and Masked), Brown Booby performs most of its chores within a couple of miles of land.

Frigatebirds. Family Fregatidae

Of five species known in the world, only one has been documented as having visited the nearshore Pacific. Possessing a greater wingspan to body weight ratio than any other kind of bird, these are perfect gliders that can kite on motionless wings for very long time periods. They are known for occasional long-distance vagrancy, riding effortlessly on Earth's long winds, so

Brown Boobies (p. 104). Top: *adult (Jack Swenson)* Middle: *adult pair. Male, left; female, right. (Bernie Tershy and Craig Strong)* Bottom: *immature. (Ron LeValley)*

another species or two may someday be detected gliding high along our coast.

Perhaps what keeps frigatebirds from *frequently* venturing far from their tropical homes is that boobies and pelagic terns abound there. These are birds that catch fish, which the plundering frigatebirds easily pirate away in mid-air. In more temperate latitudes, there are far fewer host species, ones that fly around carrying fish in their bills or crops. As scavengers, frigatebirds also snatch food directly from the water's surface in their long, hook-tipped bills. During these fancy maneuvers their plumage remains dry.

Frigatebirds do not like to sit on the water, may be unable to swim, and with their tiny feet are hopeless at trying to walk on land. When not in the air, they use high, exposed perches for resting and roosting (at nesting sites, the tops of highest bushes). To "take off" is sometimes inappropriate terminology for frigatebirds, as they often just unfold immense wings and rise.

Frigatebirds are also known as Man-of-War Birds.

Magnificent Frigatebird
(Fregata magnificens)

Rare, but found each year along the coast of Southern California (and at the Salton Sea) and almost each year along the Central California coast, where there are over 40 records. Though the species is extremely rare north of San Francisco, there are three records from the northern Gulf of Alaska and many in between. The numbers found vary from year to year, and since frigatebirds are so easily seen, a single bird coursing up the beach could be responsible for several records. Most have occurred in July and August, with a range of normal visitation from June to October. There are fewer than ten winter-spring records north of Baja. Some or many of the extralimital and out-of-season reports may actually pertain to the very similar Great Frigatebird, which is wide-ranging in the Pacific.

Identification. As a group, frigatebirds are unmistakable, with their very long, extremely narrow wings, deeply forked tails, and habit of seeming to be directly overhead at all times. The field guides show the difference between male, female, and immature plumages. Because Magnificent is the only species yet recorded here, one would have a good chance of being correct in calling *any* frigatebird that, but the Great Frigatebird *(Fregata minor)* breeds off western Mexico and is expected to be documented someday above the international border. In addition to tricky plumage differences, a couple of structural features may be helpful. The Great has a smaller, usually blue-gray bill compared to Magnificent's, which is longer and whiter. The Great is subtly stockier and not as angular as the rangy, stretched-out Magnificent.

Behavior. Frigatebirds are the world's most excellent gliders and, when conditions are right, may fly for days without a wing stroke. Hot air rising above islands and headlands, or sometimes open desert, provides lift for these lightweight, structurally perfect birds. When there is flapping, it is deep and appears to take place in slow motion. Magnificents are so aerial that they accomplish all foraging on-the-wing, either by snatching items from the water surface with their long hooked bills or pirating from pelicans, boobies, gulls, or terns. Not usually found far seaward (Great Frigatebirds are more pelagic), they roost on snags, bushes, or towers on land, or else just hang there, in the sky.

Magnificent Frigatebird (p. 106), immature. (Ron LeValley)

Top: *Red Phalarope (p. 109), first-winter plumage. (David Wimpfheimer)* Inset: *Red Phalarope, dorsal view. (Richard Webster)* Bottom: *Red-necked Phalarope (p. 110), juvenile plumage. (Mike Danzenbaker)*

Phalaropes. Family Scolopacidae

All three of the world's species of phalaropes are common migrants along the coast, but only two, the Red-necked and the Red, are regular offshore. The third, Wilson's Phalarope, prefers protected areas onshore and, in more general terms, the interior of western North America.

Phalaropes are really sandpipers that have become modified through the ages (with buoyant bodies, extra body feathers, and lobed swimming toes) for life upon the water rather than at its edge. Individuals sometimes spin in tight circles, drawing subsurface invertebrates toward them to pick off with quick jabs of their sharp bills. (Since most Red-necked and Red phalaropes winter south of the Equator, do you suppose each one spins in the opposite direction while there?)

Another curious fact about phalaropes is their gender role reversal. In the breeding season, females possess much more colorful and ornate plumages than do the males. They court the males and defend nesting territories on the edges of northern ponds against other females. The nest itself is a bare scrape, prepared by the female, which later may be lined with grasses. Although it is still necessary for the female to lay the eggs, all of the incubation and care and feeding of the young are the job of the male. Many females, especially Red-necked and Wilson's, depart their nest territories before the eggs are hatched, leaving all domestic duties to the males.

Red Phalarope
(Phalaropus fulicaria)

A very common spring and fall migrant offshore, with normally only a few seen on the coast. In some winters the species is fairly common offshore, and in others it is rare or absent. Occasionally, in fall, thousands are blown onshore by northwest gales, and individuals then might be found many miles inland. Otherwise, it is our most pelagic "shorebird."

Ocean Birds

The bulk of Red Phalaropes in spring pass during May, when as many as half a million have been counted in a single day passing coastal points. This, of course, is when they are dressed in their fancy rusty-red plumages. Their fall passage is much longer and extends from early September (adults first) through mid-November, with the surge of young birds swelling the ranks in late September and early October.

Identification. Generally chunkier than Red-necked Phalarope, with a distinctly bigger head, shorter, thicker neck, and shorter, stouter bill. The body is more robust and circular. Birds in spring plumage should be unmistakable. In fall, the back is pale uniform gray, darkening to blackish narrowly up the back of the neck. The black smudge behind the eye in some birds may be lacking in others, and contrary to what some field guides suggest, juvenile and winter adults have wholly black (not yellow) bills. The white wing stripe is more flashing in Red than in Red-necked, especially on the dorsal innerwing. This is a good feature to use in figuring ratios in mixed flocks. The basic call is a series of *pink* notes, slightly more drawn out and louder than the notes of Red-necked.

Behavior. See Red-necked Phalarope, as Reds, when passing California at sea, act in much the same way.

Red-necked Phalarope
(Phalaropus lobatus)

A very common spring and fall migrant on- and offshore. Often seen in large flocks at sea (350,000 were estimated moving north past Point Lobos on 8 May 1965), sometimes mixed with Red Phalaropes. The bulk in spring pass from late April through mid-May and, in fall, July through mid-October. The species is very rare offshore in summer and virtually absent from the North Pacific during winter.

Identification. Although other kinds of shorebirds often migrate up to a few miles west of the beach, Red-necked and Red phalaropes are the only ones able to sustain life at sea. They swim and feed on the water. Red-necked is thinner in all respects than Red Phalarope. Its head is smaller, its neck is thinner, and its bill is more pointed. In basic plumage the back is generally darker gray (black with two converging tan stripes in juveniles) than in Red, and the black crown, hindneck, and eye stripe are much more obvious. The white wing stripe is more narrow in Red-necked than in Red, especially on the dorsal innerwing. The basic calls are a detached series of staccato *pik* or *kik* notes, similar to but flatter than those of Red.

Behavior. Phalaropes, when not in earnest travel, move in swirling flocks, sometimes allowing themselves to blow about in the wind. When feeding, they swim, sometimes in a spinning motion, and pick invertebrates from the surface. They often occur at smooth patches of water (slicks) and along foam lines where currents merge or where wind pushes together an edge of small debris.

Notes. Formerly known here as Northern Phalarope. The name was changed to agree with the British vernacular. Intertional language is a noble notion, but our Red Phalarope was not changed to the British Gray Phalarope, so we are now stuck with Red and Red-necked.

Jaegers and Skuas. Family Laridae

Because there is disagreement about the taxonomy of skuas, the number of species in this group varies among sources from six to eight. For jaegers, all three of the world's species are regular over the nearshore Pacific, and so is one skua, the South Polar.

This is a small family, and individuals are usually scarce and solitary. Still, they are prominent players in the watery wilderness. Most of their food is physically extracted from other bird species, often during one-sided, aerial "dogfights" but also as the result of violent confrontations that occasionally end in the death of the victim. This is known as kleptoparasitism, a fancy way of saying food-stealing or pirating.

In addition to being pirates, these birds also assume the role of raptor, chasing and devouring any migrant landbird, bat, or moth unfortunate enough to overshoot the coast. During their short, high-latitude nesting season, jaegers' main diet is rodents and songbirds.

The three jaeger species nest exclusively in and near the Arctic, move south along the nearshore Eastern Pacific in fall, and return north in spring. South Polar Skuas nest in the Antarctic, and some (mostly in fall) come all the way to the North Pacific, where swarms of roaming shearwaters, which skuas pirate, spend much of their at-sea year.

Ocean Birds

Top: *South Polar Skua (p. 113).* (*Jon Winter*) Inset: *South Polar Skua, dorsal view. Note bold white wing flashes.* (*Richard Webster*)
Middle and bottom: *Pomarine Jaeger (p. 114).* (*Mike Danzenbaker*)

South Polar Skua
(Catharacta maccormicki)

A scarce migrant offshore. Most records fall between early August and late October, but some are also scattered from April through July. Like its small relatives, the jaegers, South Polar Skua is most often found where large numbers of shearwaters and gulls congregate to feed. Skuas, too, are pirates that pound other ocean birds into giving up their food. A powerful brute with great presence, a skua in its pelagic domain is always a thrill to encounter.

Identification. A big, thick-set, dark brown (true of most birds here), gull-like bird with striking, large white patches in the outerwing above and below. Dark-phase Pomarine Jaegers are sometimes misidentified as skuas, but seldom if ever is the reverse true. Skuas' fearless, rowdy energy and sheer physical bulk give this observer a spinal chill that helps identify the vision. Though jaegers are very nice, the feeling of a visual connection with them is not the same. Adult South Polar Skuas show pale, buffy orange feathering around the back of the neck that is lacking in young birds. The thick, short bill, the legs, and feet are black. South Polar Skua is a polymorphic species, but the vast majority of individuals that visit the Northeast Pacific are in the dark phase described here.

Behavior. Rarely seen from shore, skuas may be found anywhere offshore, especially near feeding shearwaters, but sometimes miles from any other bird. On a lucky day, several skuas might be seen, but they are solitary marauders here and do not flock with others of their kind except by accident. Skuas are not gentle when extracting food from victims. They may grab a shearwater's head, wing, or tail and shake and kick the bird until it vomits. We have seen skuas land on a sitting shearwater's back and push it underwater again and again. Certainly some victims die as a result of the encounter. Skua flight is direct, with heavy flapping and little gliding. Unlike jaegers, skuas seldom fly more than a few yards above the surface of the sea.

Notes. The birds we see were born in Antarctica and reared on penguin meat.

In the beginning . . . God gave man dominion over the fishes that swim in the sea and fowl that fly in the air . . . only the skua did not get the message for she lived too far away.
— South Georgia legend

Pomarine Jaeger

(Stercorarius pomarinus)

This is the jaeger most commonly seen on one-day boat trips off California. Though Parasitic Jaeger is much more frequent along the shore and inside estuaries, its favored travel path is within 1 or 2 miles offshore. The Pomarine's zone at sea seems to be from about 2 to 50 miles, dependent much upon shearwater presence. (From 20 to 50 miles west, watch also for Long-taileds, along the corridor used by Arctic Terns.) Like the other jaegers, Pomarines are pirates that bludgeon gulls and shearwaters into vomiting partially digested fish and squid, which they then ingest.

Pomarine's fall passage is more protracted than that of Parasitic, lasting from mid-July to mid-November. Some few remain through winter, when Pomarine is usually the only species to be found. In spring, most pass from mid-April through May. Nonbreeders are occasionally seen during the summer.

Identification. Largest of the three jaegers, Pomarine is big-headed, thick-necked, and heavy-chested. The wings are broad, especially at the base, and there are five to eight white-shafted primaries that show as a large white patch in the outerwing. The whole tail is shorter-based than in the smaller two species, and the elongated pair of central tail feathers are blunt-tipped even during early growth. The tips of the long central tail feathers are twisted to vertical, giving them a unique circular look when viewed from the side. The underwing coverts may show a double dark "comma," which is unique. Entirely dark individuals occur but are far outnumbered by light ones. In light-phase birds, sexual dimorphism may be indicated in the dark breast band, with females having broad and solid ones, males more narrow and spotty ones.

Behavior. Migrants and searching birds are high fliers, often first seen far above the horizon. Shearwaters are the most frequent victims of their wrath. Like other jaegers, when Pomarines fly low their flight is direct, with near constant flapping rarely interrupted by short glides or shrug-preening (see Long-tailed Jaeger), and with little or no arcing even in wind.

Parasitic Jaeger
(Stercorarius parasiticus)

This is the jaeger most often seen from land, as most migrant individuals move very near the coast. They enter bays, estuaries, and river mouths in search of small gulls and terns, which they terrorize into regurgitating their food. Though often seen along the beach and within a couple of miles west, Parasitic is decidedly less common than Pomarine offshore. Parasitic is the jaeger most often found inland.

Fall passage is from early July through early October, with heaviest flow during August. In spring most birds pass in April. They are rare or absent in most winters, when Pomarine Jaeger is more expected.

Identification. Larger than Long-tailed and smaller than Pomarine, Parasitic Jaeger is also intermediate in bulk, flight manner, and (normally) the number of white-shafted primaries (three to five). Its shape is most like Long-tailed, with narrow-based wings, a small head, and thin chest. The whole tail of both species is very long compared to that of Pomarine, and the elongated central pair of rectrices in Parasitic are pointed. (Juvenile Long-taileds have newly growing central rectrices that are blunt; Parasitics have pointed ones.) Parasitics are generally darker and browner than the pale gray Long-taileds. The upperparts of adult Parasitics are dark chocolate brown, as is the whole body of dark-phase birds, and many immatures have warm brown to cinnamon hues in the plumage, lacking in either of the other species. Most Parasitics lack the double dark "commas" on the underwing coverts that are shown by many Pomarines.

Behavior. Often seen from shore or within a mile or two west, pirating small gulls or terns. In fall in California, Elegant Terns seem to be the current favored host. Though occasional high fliers are encountered, Parasitics are mostly seen slicing along low over the waves, in a direct line, with no arcing and only occasional gliding. Shrug-preening is common (see Long-tailed Jaeger). Parasitic Jaegers always seem to be in a hurry to fly away and like other jaegers stir up trouble wherever they can find it.

Top left: *Parasitic Jaeger (p. 115), adult. (David Wimpfheimer)* Top
right: *Parasitic Jaeger, immature. (Richard Webster)* Bottom:
Long-tailed Jaeger (p. 117), subadult. (David Leal) Inset: *Long-
tailed Jaeger, adult. (Dorothy Crumb)*

Long-tailed Jaeger
(Stercorarius longicaudus)

Generally rare very nearshore and, unlike the other two jaegers, almost never seen from land. Passage of Long-tailed Jaegers is mostly beyond the continental shelf along the corridor used by Arctic Terns and Sabine's Gulls, which they pirate for food. Their southward migration past California occurs from mid-July through mid-October, and northbound from mid-April to early June. There are a couple of mid-summer records, but the species has yet to be found between November and April.

Identification. The smallest of the world's jaegers. Adults, with their extremely long, flexible, pointed tail feathers, their clearly isolated black caps, and their immaculate white chests, are easy. Some immatures may not be safely separable from same-age Parasitics or even Pomarines, but they do fly more gracefully, even ternlike, are more uniform gray above, and usually have only two white-shafted outer primaries (thus virtually no white wing patch). Unlike the other two species, some juvenile Long-taileds are pale-headed. Although their elongated central tail feathers become pointed, they are blunt-tipped during earliest growth. The dorsal light grayness, contrasting a black trailing edge to the wing, is indicative of Long-tailed Jaeger for young as well as adult birds. The bill is quite small, but so is that of some Parasitics. Wings are narrow-based compared to Pomarine, which has broad-based wings that taper toward the wrist.

Behavior. Truly pelagic, Long-tailed Jaegers escort their hosts, Arctic Terns, to the South Pacific for winter. When actually migrating or looking for a small gull or tern to beat up, they fly quite high, about 200 yards up, and are often first seen far overhead. When they are chasing or moving to a specific place, flight is low over the water and direct, with constant wingbeating and little gliding or arcing. Sometimes their flapping is interrupted for an in-flight shrug-preen, which is usually performed after some altercation. The bird raises to about 50 feet above the water, stops flapping, and shudders its body from front to back, shuffling each feather track back to its proper position.

Because many species of gulls abound along the mainland coast, they are familiar, at least generically, to most people. A few species, however, are truly pelagic during their nonbreeding season, seldom if ever visiting land. Gulls that do spend their winters at sea are small ones, able to glean survival fare from wee organisms at the water's surface. Larger species of gulls might have a hard time finding enough to scavenge on the open ocean.

Bonaparte's Gull
(Larus philadelphia)

A common spring and fall migrant, with many remaining to winter at select localities. A few young birds stay through summer. The species' heaviest spring passage is April through mid-May, and its fall passage is mid-October through mid-November. Bonaparte's Gulls nest mostly in the Canadian Arctic and Alaska, and most winter from Southern California south to northern South America.

Identification. A tiny gull that often looks more like a tern than like the larger gulls. Its outer primaries are white, showing as an immaculate wedge and contrasting the rest of the mantle (back and open upperwing). The bill is black, and the legs and feet are pinkish. In spring the head is black.

Behavior. Bonaparte's Gulls are usually gregarious, traveling in scattered groups or in tight flocks, sometimes numbering over 1,000 individuals. When foraging, they course back and forth, picking items from the water's surface while in flight.

Notes. Bonaparte's Gulls nest up to 30 feet high in coniferous trees of the far north.

Black-legged Kittiwake
(Rissa tridactyla)

Basically an offshore, wintering species, but irregular in occurrence; some years abundant and some practically absent. Black-legged Kittiwake is seldom found onshore but is sometimes common there following strong northwest gales. After winters of abundance, a few stragglers may stay through spring and summer. Usually these are immatures that could use a good molt to look happier. A few Black-leggeds may appear as early as October, but even in "flight years" the bulk of them do not arrive before mid-November or even early December. (On 24 December 1967, 20,000 were estimated present on Monterey Bay!) Usually most are gone by early April, but following "invasions," good numbers may be seen moving north well into May.

Identification. These are small gulls. Winter adults have unmarked, greenish-yellow bills, a smudge of gray from behind the eye across the nape, black legs and feet, and solid black, "dipped-in-ink" wingtips that, unlike any other *adult gull's*, lack white apical spots. (Some second-winter Ring-billed and Mew gulls or third-winter California and Western gulls retain all-black primaries, and thus vaguely resemble adult Black-leggeds.) First-winter Black-legged Kittiwakes are striking, with broad black leading edges to their otherwise gray-and-white dorsal wings, a black nuchal collar (sometimes double), and black-tipped white notched tail. The wings of Black-leggeds appear more rounded than other gulls, and the wing beats are faster and more rigid.

Sabine's Gull is also a small pelagic gull with a lovely wing pattern, vaguely similar to that of immature Black-legged Kittiwake. Immature Red-legged Kittiwakes (a species overdue but as yet unrecorded in the California Pacific) have a wing pattern and flight style intermediate between those of Sabine's Gulls and Black-legged Kittiwakes. Watching for Red-legged Kittiwakes offshore in winter will eventually be fruitful.

Behavior. More comfortable in marine than terrestrial environments, this is one of the few true sea gulls.

Notes. Black-legged Kittiwakes with pink or even reddish legs do occur. Not many, but some. Now that's hardly fair, is it?

Red-legged Kittiwake
(*Rissa brevirostris*)

Though not yet documented as having occurred in the California Pacific, this small, highly pelagic gull has been recorded south from its home range in the Bering Sea rarely to Oregon and, exceptionally, to Nevada! The world range is small, as is the world population. All nesting takes place from the Pribilof to the Komandorskiye islands (which are at the Soviet end of the Aleutians), plus a few spots in the Aleutians.

Young gulls. Top: *Black-legged Kittiwake (p. 118).* Middle:
Red-legged Kittiwake (p. 119). Bottom: *Sabine's Gull (p. 122).*
(Keith Hansen)

Most individuals winter in, or just south of, the breeding range, well away from land. Your best chance of seeing one of these lovely birds is to fly to Saint Paul from Anchorage in summer and peek over the edge of the cliff.

Identification. These are small gulls with incredible beauty. Adults have bright, tomato-red legs and feet, which are absolutely diagnostic if seen. Unfortunately the legs and feet are pretty much concealed when the birds are flying or sitting on the water. The bill is unmarked yellow and unusually short. These features, complemented by the very round forecrown and large, dark eyes, give the species an exceptionally cute facial expression, even more than that of Black-legged Kittiwake or Mew Gull. Additionally, adults differ from Black-legged in having uniform dark mantles (there is a distinct paling in Black-legged at the base of the primaries between the wrist and the black tips); a less "dipped in ink" look to the black primary tips; a broader white trailing edge to the uppwerwing; and, from below, a gray wash inside the trailing edge and throughout the outerwing surface. The wings themselves are shorter and broader, and the wing beats are more rapid.

Immature Red-legged Kittiwakes look more like their adults than Black-leggeds do theirs. With their all-white tails (unique in the first winter to this species), fairly uniform dark mantles, and extensive black wingtips, immature Red-leggeds are unlike first- (or second!) winter Black-leggeds, which are much more highly patterned. Young Red-leggeds do have one or two gray nuchal collars and bills that turn from black to yellow during their first autumn. In these ways they are like Black-leggeds of the same age.

Young Red-leggeds show a white wedge on the dorsal wing surface tapering from the broad white trailing edge to a point posterior to the wrist. With the gray back and dorsal innerwing, the white midwing triangle, and the blackish outerwing, the pattern is quite similar to that of Sabine's Gull.

Sabine's Gull is a migrant through the nearshore Pacific and should be absent in winter from December through March. If a bird is seen during that period that *looks* like a Sabine's Gull, make sure it is not an immature Red-legged Kittiwake.

Behavior. True sea gulls, Red-legged Kittiwakes only associate with land to nest. They are as oceanic as Black-legged Kittiwakes, or more so. Shy and usually solitary at sea, individuals are only occasionally attracted to boats for forage.

Sabine's Gull

(Xema sabini)

An uncommon offshore migrant spring and fall. Spring passage is mid-April through May, peaking in early May. Fall passage is more broadly protracted and lasts from late July through early November, peaking in September. Truly oceanic, this fine bird is seldom seen from shore or onshore, and the migration corridor it uses is generally between 10 and 100 miles seaward. Although Sabine's Gulls are sometimes encountered in large numbers (as many as 1,000 off Monterey on 1 October 1966), few or none is a more usual tally.

Identification. An especially beautiful gull, easily identified at any age by its striking wing pattern. Sabine's Gulls are very buoyant and ternlike in flight. When sitting on the water they ride high, and the long primaries stick well out, beyond the tail.

Bonaparte's Gulls and immature Black-legged Kittiwakes are somewhat similar. Immature Red-legged Kittiwakes (not yet recorded for California) have a very similar wing pattern. Because Sabine's Gulls should be absent from the California Pacific in winter, anything that looks like one in that season should be carefully scrutinized.

Behavior. Sabine's Gulls usually travel in small parties or scattered flocks, but singles are sometimes found. They are occasionally attracted to a bird flock following a boat, but they never stay very long.

Notes. Breeds circumpolarly in the high Arctic and winters at sea, well below the Equator.

Top: *Red-legged Kittiwake (p. 119), winter adult. (Bernie Tershy and Dawn Breese)* Bottom left: *Sabine's Gull (p. 122), spring adult. (Ed Harper)* Bottom right: *Sabine's Gull, first autumn. (Mike Danzenbaker)*

Heermann's Gull
(Larus heermanni)

Except for one nesting record from Alcatraz Island in San Francisco Bay, this species nests entirely south of our region, but northward postbreeding dispersal causes its common appearance from late June through November. More individuals occur south than north, and Bodega Harbor is usually the northern limit of true abundance. Heermann's Gulls are very agile, usually outcompeting other birds for tidbits of chum. They often hang out with Brown Pelicans, which they escort north from Baja, and they snatch bits of food spilling out of the pelicans' bills. Heermann's Gulls with distinct, symmetrical, white patches in the outerwings occur, perhaps 1 in 200.

Mew Gull
(Larus canus)

This delicate, small gull is common from late October through early April and rare or absent at other times. Mew Gulls come to us from the north, and their winter range ends abruptly in southernmost California. Thus they are more common off the northern part of the state.

Ring-billed Gull
(Larus delawarensis)

This species, though common and easy to find onshore, hates the ocean, and it is rare at any season (most records are from late summer to early fall) to find one in the swarm behind an offshore boat.

California Gull
(Larus californicus)

Abundant from early August through April and uncommon in summer. Often the second most common gull (after Western Gull) seen on trips to 20 miles seaward.

Herring Gull
(Larus argentatus)

Common offshore from late October through March and rare at other seasons. Because of field guide inaccuracies, this species may be confused with the light-mantled northern race of Western Gull. Birds of this sort off California from mid-April to late September *are* Westerns. Both species are common along the coast the rest of the year. Hybrids of Herring with Glaucous or Glaucous-winged gulls have been documented for California, on- and offshore.

Thayer's Gull
(Larus thayeri)

Uncommon from late October through March, but often seen during that period in the swarm behind boats. The classification of this bird has long been enigmatic. Formerly considered part of Herring Gull, it seems likely that the species will eventually be lumped with Iceland Gull. In any case, this kind of bird nests in the Canadian Arctic and presumably migrates southwesterly overland, with few if any stopovers, to winter on the west coast of North America.

Western Gull
(Larus occidentalis)

Common to abundant throughout the year, this species is quite sedentary and breeds along the California coast. There are two races that are sometimes identifiable in the field. Nesters from Monterey south (*L. o. wymani*) are dark mantled. Northernmost examples of the northern race (*L. o. occidentalis*) are distinctly paler. The gray backs of southern-

Ocean Birds

nesting birds of *occidentalis,* though, are more similar to those of *wymani.* In winter, *wymani* have gray streaks on the hindcrown and nape. From San Francisco north, winter Westerns are entirely white-headed. Winter adults of all other gull species in the range have extensive gray head streaking. This species is common at sea, out to 70 miles.

Glaucous-winged Gull
(Larus glaucescens)

Common from mid-October through March and rare from May through September. The few summering birds are sick or lazy and don't go adventuring offshore. Glaucous-wingeds breed in Washington and British Columbia and are much more numerous off Northern than Southern California, which is the southward limit of their normal distribution.

Western × Glaucous-winged Gull Hybrid
(Larus occidentalis × glaucescens)

A fairly common intergrade showing characteristics intermediate between the two parent types. Adults with a pale mantle, like Glaucous-winged, and black primary tips, like Western, superficially resemble Herring and Thayer's gulls, so think carefully. In some areas of the Puget Sound region, where the two are sympatric breeders merging into one phenotype, few individuals are identifiable as either kind. Some experienced gull-watchers jokingly refer to the whole assemblage there as "*Larus pugetensis.*" Like other kinds of Northern Hemisphere gulls (Glaucous, Herring, Iceland, and Thayer's), these birds do not conform to our rules of specification when their summer ranges collide.

Glaucous Gull
(Larus hyperboreus)

A rare visitor from November through March, but many of the records are offshore. There are a few records from April through May and in October. Caution, however, is urged. In other species of gulls, individuals that lack the energy to migrate also lack the energy to molt, and as the old feathers become more and more abraded they become more white. This is especially true for Glaucous-winged and Thayer's gulls. Partial albinism is also relatively frequent in gulls. Bill size and pattern on first- and second-year Glaucous Gulls must be noted before an identification may be clinched.

Terns. Family Laridae

Terns are gull-like birds that live near aquatic habitats, including the ocean. Unlike gulls, they feed by plunge-diving headlong into the water after small surface fish. Some (Caspian, Elegant, and Forster's) are inshore species seldom roaming farther than the sight of land, whereas others (Arctic and Common) are very much pelagic.

Caspian Tern
(Sterna caspia)

Very common from mid-March into October, with more birds south than north. Caspian Tern is locally present in winter along the Southern California coast at the few remaining natural estuaries, other wetlands, and beaches north to at least Point Mugu, Ventura County. Caspian Terns cling to the coast and are very rarely encountered more than a wee distance offshore.

Royal and Elegant terns are similar. The Caspian Tern is larger and heavier in all regards than Royal or Elegant and shows bolder black underwing tips (all primaries). Caspian's bill is Oyster-catcher red, redder than the carrot-orange bills of the other two, and usually shows a smudge of gray or black on the tip that is lacking in the two smaller species'. Caspian's usual call is a very distinctive, loud, single-syllabled, low and raspy *kaaup* or *cowup*, most unlike the higher, more squeaky *errik* or *erreek* of Elegant and similar utterances of Royal.

Top: *Common Tern (p. 129)*. *(Ed Harper)* Inset: *Arctic Tern (p. 129)*, *first winter*. *(Mike Danzenbaker)* Bottom: *Arctic Tern, adult*. *(Ed Harper)*

Common Tern

(Sterna hirundo)

A common fall and spring migrant nearshore, and individuals or small groups regularly occur onshore — at beaches, river mouths, and harbors or within the boundaries of larger estuaries and bays. The species is virtually absent from California in winter except at San Diego, where in some years a few individuals remain in that season (up to 15 during winter 1974–75). A few non-breeders may remain through summer in special places like Moss Landing and south San Diego Bay (175 there on 4 July 1962). Spring passage occurs entirely between mid-April and late May. As with most long-distance north-south migrants near the California coast, fall passage is more broadly protracted, extending from mid-July through October.

Identification. See Arctic Tern, below, and *Field Characteristics of Small Terns*, page 134.

Behavior. Like the other small terns, Commons are quite aerial, rarely landing on the water (but occasionally landing on kelp paddies or floating debris). They carry out foraging by high flying, seeing small surface fish, and diving headlong into the sea, most often retrieving the target.

Although sometimes found in mixed flocks, Common Terns generally migrate along a corridor slightly shoreward from that used by Arctic Terns (e.g., in 23 years of daily watching from Southeast Farallon Island there are only three records for Common and many hundreds for Arctic). Commons frequently come onshore to preen and stand around, often in the company of Forster's Terns. Healthy Arctic Terns seldom appear on land away from their Arctic nesting range.

Arctic Tern

(Sterna paradisaea)

A common fall and scarce spring migrant well offshore, 10 to 40 miles. It is likely that Arctic Tern's spring migration route is mostly farther seaward, in the "unknown zone" 40 to 200 miles out. The main timing of spring passage here is early May, and fall passage takes place from mid-July into mid-October. It is rare to find an Arctic Tern on the mainland, and individuals that do end up on the beach are usually sick, oiled, or confused.

Identification. Most like Common Tern but even more delicate than that species. Arctic Terns have shorter bills and more rounded heads than Common and Forster's and, in adults, much longer tails. This gives Arctics a unique shape, with the part of the bird in front of the leading edge of the wing much shorter than the part behind the trailing edge. For adults of the other two species, the front and back ends are more equal. Arctics of all ages also have translucent primaries through which much light may pass, and the trailing edge of the outerwing is narrowly and evenly margined with black. Common's wings are much more opaque, and the black trailing edge to the outerwing is wedge-shaped and less well defined.

The bills of adult Arctics are usually blood red to the tip and those of the others dark-tipped, but there are exceptions, such as Common Terns with all-reddish-orange bills. The legs *(tarsi)* of Arctics are distinctly shorter than those of Common, and given comparable conditions Arctics stand noticeably shorter, showing very little leg. This may come in handy for identifying immatures standing on floating logs or kelp paddies.

Behavior. Very graceful and buoyant fliers, Arctic Terns at sea are seldom encountered on the water. They view small fish and other organisms from above and capture them by plunge-diving into the water.

Notes. When Long-tailed Jaegers are found in this region, they are often near migrating Arctic Terns. During the nonbreeding season jaegers pirate food from terns up and down the world.

Arctic Terns are famous as long-distance migrants. Nesting in the high Arctic from April into July, they migrate all the way south to Antarctic waters, where they spend their nonbreeding period during the austral summer. This 22,000-mile annual round-trip allows them to spend essentially their whole lives in "good weather," and given the very long periods of daylight during summer near both poles, they probably spend a larger portion of their lives in sunlight than any other living organism.

Forster's Tern
(Sterna forsteri)

V ery common in summer and locally common (more so in Southern than Northern California) in winter along the coast itself. Extremely rare more than a couple of miles west of the mainland (there is only one Farallon record, 28 October 1986), so terns of this type encountered offshore will almost always be Arctic or Common terns.

Royal Tern
(Sterna maxima)

L ocally fairly common in *winter* (October into February) from San Simeon south, becoming most evident at San Diego Bay. It is the tern most often seen near the Channel Islands (where it is often mistaken by the overenthusiastic for a tropicbird), and some nonbreeders summer there, as they do at San Diego. Elsewhere in California, Royal Tern is absent in summer. Elegant Terns, abundant on the coast in summer, are sometimes mistaken for Royals.

Royal Tern is now a rare species in Northern California but was formerly common in winter at least to San Francisco. It is now only rarely reported, and most of the few records for the last 40 years are form the Monterey Bay area in autumn.

Elegant Tern
(Sterna elegans)

A common late summer and fall visitor north to Sonoma County, California, and uncommon north of there. For this warm-water species, the extent of its northward dispersal may be regulated by the sea surface temperatures. During the El Niño of 1982–1983, Elegant Terns performed a major northward surge, with hundreds in Oregon and small groups appearing up the coast to Vancouver, B.C. (21 August 1983) and Victoria (the following day). These were the first records for British Columbia and Canada. Although Elegant Terns nest at San Diego Bay and in Orange County, many more come north along the coast from Mexico from late June into early November.

Top: *Royal Tern (p. 131). (Mike Danzenbaker)* Bottom: *Elegant Tern (p. 131). (Rich Stallcup)*

They are very rare well offshore but are quite obvious as part of the avifauna in harbors and bays and up to two miles seaward. Their startling, high, grating *erreek* call is an easy vocalization to learn and can be heard at great distances. They are often the target of pirating attacks by Parasitic Jaegers.

Identification. Larger than the "small terns" and smaller and narrower than Caspian Tern. The bill is long, thin, and carrot-orange, a feature shared only with Royal Tern. Birds seen north of Bolsa Chica or after June are in winter plumage, with broadly white forecrowns and shaggy black hindcrowns that extend narrowly forward to include the eye.

Royal Terns are slightly larger in all respects, and this is especially noticeable in perched, mixed flocks, where Royals are taller. Bills of both species are orange, but that of Royal is relatively shorter, thicker, and less drooped at the tip. Royal's color, on average, is whiter than Elegant's in the wingtips and about the heads of nonbreeding birds (both species are in "winter" plumage most of the year). Whereas black from the nape of Elegant Tern lines around to include the eye, in Royal Tern the eye stands alone in the white, forward of that line. The call of Royal is similar to that of Elegant but lower in pitch and not as well broadcast.

Behavior. Though very social at rest (sitting in large tight flocks on sandbars or kelp), Elegant Terns scatter when feeding. Their foraging sequence involves high flight (50 to 200 yards), spotting small surface fish, and plunging headlong into the water, usually with successful results.

Notes. Many insatiable young Elegant Terns (one per adult), fully capable of feeding themselves, follow parents from Mexico north and back again, constantly nagging and begging for food.

Field Characteristics of Small Terns

Field identification of *Sterna* terns: The identification of immatures, and many times of adults, is difficult and can be impossible under less than optimum viewing conditions. Field guides disagree, and popular consensus is usually inaccurate, concerning certain identification clues for these fine birds.

Forster's Tern is the most distinct of these three similar species, so let us look at it contrasted with Common and Arctic, or "Commic," terns. Common and Arctic terns are superficially quite similar, but posture and coloration differences make them easily separable under good viewing conditions.

Forster's

- Adult's mantle is pale gray, and tail is pale grayish, yielding little contrast on upperpart (not valid in immature).
- Adult has distinctly white outer web to outer tail feathers (tail grayish).
- Adult's primaries are lighter than mantle above and uniformly light from below.
- In winter and immature birds, only the auriculars are black and are seen as a black teardrop-shaped patch behind the eye. The nape is unmarked white.
- Immature has white leading edges to the innerwings.

- Immature has buff edges to its back feathers, black tips to its outer three rectrices, and black-tipped primaries (from below), like Common Tern.
- Wing beats (flying at ease) are relatively shallow and fast.
- When bird is perched, wingtips fall short of the end of the tail.

"Commic"

- Adult's mantle is darker gray than Forster's. White rump and tail yield distinct back-tail contrast (as in immature Forster's).
- Adult has distinctly dark outer web to outer tail feathers (tail white).
- Adult's primaries are as dark or darker than mantle above and show black tips from below.
- In winter and immature birds, the eye is in the black. The black hindcrown triangles onto the nape like a bandanna worn black on white.
- Immature has dark leading edges to the innerwings, most noticeable as dark shoulder crescents on perched birds. This mark can sometimes be covered by body feathers.
- Immature has brown and black edges to its back feathers and dusky tips to outer rectrices.

- Wing beats (flying at ease) are relatively deep and slow.
- When bird is perched, wingtips meet or slightly exceed the end of the tail.

Common

- In flight, the relatively long bill and head and short tail make the part of the bird in front of the wings about the same length as the part behind the wings. (Good straight-profile view only.)
- Long bill gives the head a long, sleek appearance.
- Looking up at the bird, little or no light can be seen through the outer primaries, and the tail shows dark outer edges.

- Underside of primaries broadly tipped with dark.
- Adults in spring are flushed with light or dark gray, some nearly matching that of Arctic. No obvious white stripe on face.
- Adult's bill is usually orange-red and usually tipped with dark.

- When perched, legs (tarsi) appear quite long when compared to similarly perched Arctic Tern's but are still much shorter than those of Forster's.
- When perched, wingtips extend beyond the end of the tail.
- Dorsal wing coverts of immature are gray, with secondaries darker.
- Has a dark wedge on upperwing surface, from tip toward base of fifth and sixth primaries.

Arctic

- In flight, the relatively short bill and head and long tail make the part of the bird in front of the wings noticeably shorter than that part of the bird behind the wings.

- Short bill gives the head a rounded, delicate look.
- Looking up at the bird, much light may be seen through nearly all primary and secondary feathers, forming large triangles of transparency, and the tail is quite white all over.
- Underside of primaries narrowly tipped with blackish.
- Adults in spring are distinctly gray below but show a clearly defined white facial stripe between the black cap and the gray throat.
- Adult's bill is blood red with no dark tip (Common can look like this).
- When perched, legs (tarsi) appear quite short when compared to similarly perched Common Tern's.

- When perched, wingtips meet or fall short of the end of the tail.
- Dorsal wing coverts of immature are whitish and secondaries white.

- Lacks the black wedge on upperwing surface.

Three marks often considered to be diagnostic should be used only to qualify other evidence.

1. *Bill color* is variable. In spring, Forster's is usually yellow-orange with a dark tip, Common's is usually orange-red with a black tip, and Arctic's is usually blood-red to the tip. Forster's, however, can be quite red, and Common's can be red with no black tip. Bills of all three species turn black in winter, sometimes with a white tip recalling Sandwich Tern.

2. Apparent *tarsal length* depends on how the bird is standing and how the belly feathers are arranged.

3. The *vocalizations* of these birds vary considerably, migrants seldom call, and the field guide descriptions leave most people confounded. The differences in call seem to be of relative nasality, with the voice of the Arctic being generally harsher and more raspy than the Common's, and the Common's more raspy than the Forster's'.

Of 22 species of alcids worldwide, 15 are part of California's oceanic fauna, some as abundant residents and some as accidental visitors. That the whole family evolved in northern biomes (perhaps the Bering Sea) is the reason for their relative abundance here.

Alcids are strong, thick, short-necked birds that fly by rapid beating of their seemingly inadequate forward appendages; they look like footballs with wings. To feed, they dive from the surface and use half-open wings to propel themselves, along with their flutter-kicking webbed feet. Once below the surface, different species forage in different habitats. Some, like Rhinoceros Auklet, may dive for more than two minutes and have been incidentally captured in fishing nets at 600 feet. Others, like Pigeon Guillemot, may snip small anchovies just below the surface or forage in zones of relatively shallow water.

Common Murre

(Uria aalge)

Common (but see *Notes,* below) resident of Central and Northern California; relatively uncommon, irregular, and seasonal (mostly winter) off Southern California. When given a chance by humans, murres become an abundant nesting species on rocks and islands off the California coast. In 1980 it was estimated (Sowls) that over 360,000 birds were breeding here, with 65% off Humboldt and Del Norte counties and 17% at the Farallones. (Before 1800 there may have been 400,000 Common Murres on the Farallones alone, but egg harvesting and "incidental killing" from then until 1967 have kept numbers very low). Away from nesting colonies (when the population is high), murres are sometimes found swimming in large numbers very near the coast and, normally, offshore to perhaps ten miles. Singles, pairs (usually an adult and this-year's chick), or small groups sometimes enter bays and harbors also. Off Southern California, murres formerly nested near San Miguel Island, and the species as a whole was probably present more regularly and in larger numbers than it is today. Now the southernmost colony is at Hurricane Rocks, off the northern Big Sur coast, Monterey County.

Identification. A large black-and-white alcid (auk) with distinctive winter and summer plumages. Common differs in plumage from the very rare Thick-billed Murre in being less black (more dark gray-brown) and, in winter plumage, much whiter in the face and neck. In summer plumage, Common's white chest rounds off into the dark neck; Thick-billed's white chest tapers to a white point on the black neck. The white flanks of Common Murre are barred brownish; those of Thick-billed are unmarked. The most consistent differentiating feature is the *shape* of the bill. For Common, the culmen (dorsal edge of the upper mandible) is fairly straight in the basal half, decurving distally. The angle in the gonys (ventral edge of the lower mandible) is located less than halfway out. Thick-billed has an evenly decurved culmen, and the angle of the gonys is about halfway out. The bill of Thick-billed appears slightly shorter and thicker, but its shape, not bulk, should be noted. Common Murre chicks have shorter bills than do their parents.

Because in fall most Commons are in winter plumage, dark-headed birds should be checked as possible Thick-billeds. Juvenile Pigeon Guillemots are vaguely similar but have different plumage and posture. Very young Common Murres, which leave the nest a couple of days after hatching to grow up at sea with their dads, are small, blackish above and white below, and have been mistaken for Xantus' Murrelets. If you see a mixed pair — one Common Murre and one Xantus' Murrelet — give it some more thought.

Notes. Historically, Common Murre populations have been battered by humans for their meat and eggs. Because of their highly colonial nesting practices on islets off the coast, they were considered an easy protein "resource." Once that calamity was stopped, murre populations here made an excellent recovery but in the past 15 years have suffered a devastating one-two-three knockout combination. During the warm-water period of the 1982–1983 El Niño, they had little or no reproductive success because of a scarcity of forage fish. Oil spills, most notably from the *Puerto Rican* in November 1984, eliminated thousands, but tens or maybe hundreds of thousands of Common Murres drowned in gill nets between 1983 and 1986. Many corpses were just thrown overboard, and others were crammed into weighted 50-gallon plastic bags, some of which drifted to the beach.

Nothing can be done about the nature of fluctuating sea temperatures, but an understanding public can insist that fishermen kill only fish and that oil companies kill only mosquitoes.

Ocean Birds

Top: *Common Murre (p. 136), young chick. Note possible
confusion with murrelets (shown elsewhere). (Ann Miller)* Inset:
*Two Common Murres. Left, adult changing from summer to
winter plumage; right, first-winter chick. (Rod Norden)* Bottom:
Thick-billed Murre (p. 139), winter adult. (Rich Stallcup)

Thick-billed Murre
(Uria lomvia)

Accidental. A small flurry of records and a record or two for each year, mostly near Monterey Harbor, occurred from the mid-1960s to the mid-1970s during a period of relatively cool water. One individual, with Common Murres two miles west of Point Joe on 4 October 1981, was the only Thick-billed found there since 1975. The next was on 8 September 1989 at Monterey, and up to five were present later that month. One or two were still present into early spring 1990. An individual at the Eel River mouth in Humboldt County on 3 January 1977 and one flying south past Southeast Farallon on 29 October 1988 are the only California records away from Monterey. All these reports are for winter, August through February. In summer, Thick-billed Murres have been seen recently near Southeast Farallon (there is a huge Common Murre colony there), and on 28 June 1989 an adult leading a string of six or seven Common Murres passed Point Reyes Lighthouse heading toward the island. There are a few scattered records along the coast north to northern British Columbia, which is the southern limit of this species' normal range.

Identification. Very much like Common Murre but, plumage-for-plumage, blacker (less dark gray-brown) above. Winter birds are very dark-faced, without the broad white stripe behind the eye connecting to the white neck that is present in Common Murre. Because in the late fall *most* Common Murres are in winter plumage, dark-headed individuals should be carefully checked as possible Thick-billeds. Summer plumages are more alike, but on Thick-billed the white of the underparts comes to a *point* on the black throat; on Common, this white is more rounded. The flanks of Thick-billed Murre are unmarked white. Those of Common Murre are barred dark brown. The white tomium (inner cutting-edge of the bill) is absent or obscure on most Thick-billeds seen off California. The most consistent differentiating feature is the *shape* of the bill. Thick-billeds have an evenly decurved culmen (dorsal edge of the upper mandible), and the angle on the gonys (ventral edge of the lower mandible) is about halfway out. For Commons, the culmen is fairly straight in the basal half, decurving distally. The angle of the gonys is nearer the bird's face. The bill of Thick-billed appears slightly shorter and thicker, but its *shape*, not bulk, should be noted. Be aware that Common Murre chicks have shorter bills than their parents.

Behavior. Murres are nearshore species here, most often seen in groups on the water. Unlike guillemots, murres ride low in the water, with "closed necks," and hold their bills tilted slightly upward. Most Thick-billeds found this far south have been unwell and near Monterey Harbor's kelp line.

Notes. The birds known to us as murres are called guillemots in English-speaking Europe.

Pigeon Guillemot
(Cepphus columba)

A common summer bird from Shell Beach north, nesting on islets, islands (the northern Channel Islands and Farallones), and the mainland on cliffs, in caves, and under buildings such as along Cannery Row in Pacific Grove. Pigeon Guillemots are uncommon to rare south of Santa Barbara, and most occurrences there are the result of southerly post-breeding dispersal. A record from Los Coronados Island off northernmost Baja on 6 June 1969 is the southernmost for this species. It is very rare anywhere along the California coast in winter (late October to mid-February), though a scattered few are regularly found at special places, such as the south shore of Monterey Bay and off Bodega Head. Where they all go remains a mystery (see *Notes*, below). The first adults return to their colonies to begin breeding activities in mid-February, and all are present and busy by the end of March. After the nesting season, most guillemots are absent from the California Pacific by mid-September.

Identification. Adults are easy to identify, with their velvety black plumage broken only by immaculate dorsal wing coverts that show as a big white patch both in flight and at rest. The bright red legs and feet are color-coordinated with the mouth lining. Juveniles look vaguely like Common Murres but have different plumage and posture (guillemots hold their heads up, murres slouch) and are more frequently mistaken for Marbled Murrelets. Watch for the larger size and taller shape of the guillemot, and see that the white patch is made up of coverts for guillemot versus scapulars for murrelet.

Behavior. Seldom seen more than a half mile from the coast or from island breeding spots (about 2,000 nest on Southeast Farallon). Most guillemots found away from nests are singles, but small parties do occur. The species is not too skittish and usually can be approached closely by boat.

Notes. Pigeon Guillemots, though common in spring and summer, are virtually absent the rest of the year, and the wonderful part is that nobody knows for sure where they go. For four months of the year, most of the California population is at large. It is highly doubtful that they go *east*, as the high deserts of Nevada and Utah are not suitable for an alcid's foraging abilities, and they do not go *south* along the coast undetected, as they could not pass the legions of good observers there. To escape to the *west* (far offshore) seems unlikely because of the lack of records and the species' apparent reluctance to venture far from land while nesting. This leaves only the *north;* the California population could melt into large numbers of guillemots there, unnoticed. We will need marked California birds to be recovered on the winter water, or else to see large numbers of them in transit to be sure. Isn't that strange?

Marbled Murrelet
(Brachyramphus marmoratus)

Rare off Southern California, increasingly common north along the coast. Though still much a mystery (see *Notes,* below), these birds nest high in old-growth coniferous trees, wherever large stands remain near the shore, probably from Monterey County north. It is also probable that birds nesting here are year-round residents, although certainly there are periodic incursions of wintering birds from north of California that swell the population here. The winter of 1979–1980 saw such an event, and the species was widely reported along all of Southern California.

Identification. Summer and winter plumages are most like those of Kittlitz's Murrelet, a species rarely found south of Alaska. The two are very similar in overall shape, but the bill of

Top: *Marbled Murrelet (p. 141). (Ed Harper)* Middle: *Pigeon Guil-lemot (p. 140), first autumn. (Ed Harper)* Bottom: *Kittlitz's Mur-relet (p. 144), winter. (Tim Zurowski)*

Marbled is longer than that of Kittlitz's and more exposed from the nasal-groove feathering. Both are mottled brown in summer, but Marbled is uniform dark above, especially on the back and crown, and its color is more chocolate (and less sandy or yellow-brown). In winter, both have white scapulars that contrast like racing stripes against the blackish back and dorsal wing. Distribution of white in the face is somewhat variable, but Marbleds always have less. Some birds have different facial patterns on each side of the head, so see both sides on any suspected rarity. While Marbleds have darkish outer tail feathers, Kittlitz's have white. (Marbled's white uppertail coverts, if hanging over the base of the tail, may give the appearance of white outer tail feathers.) This feature is easily seen on birds landing or taking off, even at a long distance. A grayish necklace, common to both species in winter plumages, is mostly complete in Kittlitz's and only partial in Marbled.

Young Common Murres, only half the size of their parents, have been mistaken for murrelets. More than once we have heard reports of a mixed pair—one murre and one murrelet! Clearly these turn out to be an adult murre with a chick. Not a bad mistake—what book ever mentioned that there would be such tiny murres?

Behavior. These birds cling to the coast and, even where common, they are seldom seen more than a mile from shore. Generally they are more easily seen from shore than from ocean-going vessels. Like Craveri's and Xantus', Marbleds are most often found in twos, but they tend to be spooky, not usually allowing close approach or good views.

Notes. The nest of this species remained undiscovered in North America until 7 August 1974, when a tree worker found a chick sitting in a guano-carpeted depression on a broad Douglas fir branch 148 feet above the ground at Big Basin State Park, Santa Cruz County, California. There remain very few descriptions of actual nest sites or of behavior at the nest, here or in the Soviet Union, though the U.S. Forest Service and the U. S. Fish and Wildlife Service are closing in on the answers.

Strictly a North Pacific bird, the Marbled Murrelet has occurred at surprising inland localities, such as Mono Lake, Quebec, Massachusetts, Indiana, Arkansas, and Colorado. These vagrants have been identified as belonging to the Western Pacific Siberian population!

Kittlitz's Murrelet

(Brachyramphus brevirostris)

Very rare south of Alaska (individuals have been found only at Victoria, British Columbia, and at Friday Harbor and Port Townsend, Washington). A juvenile individual found alive on a beach at La Jolla, San Diego County, on 16 August 1969 was designated an unacceptable record by the California Bird Records Committee on grounds that, because of the early date and young age of the bird, it must have been unnaturally transported. The report was resubmitted, though, and eventually passed. It remains the only record south of northern Washington.

Identification. Summer and winter plumages are most like those of Marbled Murrelet, a much more common species in the California Pacific. The two birds are very similar in overall shape, but the bill of Kittlitz's is shorter than that of Marbled, with just a black nub exiting the exceptionally well feathered foreface. The mottled summer plumage of Kittlitz's is overall paler than Marbled's, especially in the head and back, which appear light tan or even yellowish. The outer tail feathers are white (dusky on Marbled) and easily seen, even at a distance, when the birds are taking off or landing. In winter plumage, Kittlitz's have whiter faces than Marbleds, and the pale grayish necklace is complete or nearly so. The faces of some Marbleds are whiter than those of others (and than shown in field guides), and oddly, some individuals have different patterns on either side of the head.

Behavior. Like Marbled Murrelets, Kittlitz's are quite coastal, seldom venturing to the open sea.

Notes. Nests in the Aleutians, coastal southern and western Alaska, probably the Komandorskiye Islands, and the Chuckchi Peninsula in the Soviet Union. Kittlitz's mostly winters in its nesting range.

Xantus' Murrelet
(Synthliboramphus hypoleucus)

The dark-faced northern race *(S. h. scrippsi)* is a common breeder on some of the Channel Islands (especially Santa Barbara Island) off Southern California, and most records from that area are from March through July. During June at least some of the population shifts (swims?) north, and August through early October is the peak period of occurrence off Monterey. At Monterey, Xantus' are uncommon at best and rare in winter and spring, but there are recent records from every month of the year. Recent spring sightings near Southeast Farallon and a bird found dead in a crevice in May 1971 may suggest, at least, the species' interest in nesting there.

The light-faced southern race *(S. h. hypoleucus)* is a rare and irregular fall (postbreeding) drifter from islands off southern Baja. This is clearly the rarer form to be found off California, so a record of two collected off Cape Flattery, Washington, on 7 August 1947 is curious. Not only is it the northernmost record, but the early date is odd.

Identification. Like Craveri's Murrelet, but in good light shows more slaty-black above, lacking brownish tones. Xantus' underwings are gleaming white, sometimes flecked with a few dark feathers but not *mostly* gray (as in Craveri's). Xantus' lacks the dark peninsula onto the sides of the upper breast that is present in Craveri's, and it has a slightly shorter, thicker bill. The northern race is most similar to Craveri's, and differences in pattern other than the underwings are subtle: the black of the face does not go forward past the gape to meet on the foremost chin as it does in Craveri's. This is a very small bit of feathers, and a difficult call at sea. The southern race is more distinctive, as the cheeks are more extensively white, extending up in front of the eye and occasionally over and behind it.

Top: *Museum specimens, from top to bottom: Xantus' Murrelet (p. 145), southern race (hypoleuca); Xantus' Murrelet, northern race (scripsii); Craveri's Murrelet (p. 147). (Jon Winter)* Inset: *Xantus' Murrelet. (Mike Danzenbaker)* Bottom: *Craveri's Murrelets, rocketing from water. (Dawn Breese)*

Behavior. Unlike other murrelets that swim with their necks scrunched down, Xantus' and Craveri's usually hold their heads high with necks erect. At the approach of a boat they nervously dive a lot, and if there are two birds (the usual case), they call when on the surface. Before flight (which will happen soon), these birds often "stand up" and exercise their wings. Because when they do fly they rocket from the water and quickly disappear low and away, the exercise behavior is the best time to see their underwings. It happens quickly, so watch constantly. They are sleeker in flight than auklets and take flight more easily (they do not have to run for takeoff).

Notes. At San Benitos Island off Baja, both races of Xantus' and Craveri's murrelets all breed sympatrically. There is zero or near zero mixing between Xantus' and Craveri's and limited mixing between the two Xantus' types. In this case, *scrippsi* and *hypoleucus* behave as if they were separate species.

Craveri's Murrelet
(Synthliboramphus craveri)

Irregular and at best uncommon from July through October; following "good falls" a few may remain into January. Waters off San Diego have yielded by far the most records for Southern California, and although the mid- and late eighties were poor there, it may be the northern limit of the species' normal range of occurrence. At Monterey, where 25 were collected in 1910, the species went unrecorded until the 1970s but has now been found every fall since 1977. North of San Francisco it is very rare, but there is a record from Siltcoos State Beach, Lane County, Oregon, from 15 August 1975! Water temperature patterns no doubt dictate its range. Identification problems with Xantus' Murrelet have perhaps blurred Craveri's true annual distribution status offshore California.

Identification. Like Xantus' Murrelet but (in good light) more brownish-black above, lacking slaty tones. Underwings of Craveri's are cloudy gray, sometimes with a narrow white core but never all white as in Xantus'. A wide peninsula of black intrudes from the upper back into the white sides of the breast; for Xantus' this area is evenly white. Craveri's has a slightly longer, thinner bill than Xantus', and the dark feathering from the cheeks extends forward past the gape onto the foremost chin. The chin of Xantus' is white to the bill itself, but the difference is slight and hard to see.

Behavior. Craveri's swimming behavior is similar to that of Xantus'. Unlike other murrelets, which swim with their necks scrunched down, Craveri's and Xantus' usually hold their heads high with their necks erect. At the approach of a boat, they nervously dive a lot, and if there are two birds (the usual case), they call when on the surface. Before flight (which will happen soon) these birds often "stand up" and exercise their wings. This is the best time to see their underwing patterns, so watch constantly.

At departure, unlike most alcids that pat-pat-patter away, these birds rocket themselves aloft and fly low over the water directly away for long distances. Watch them as long as possible; they may land again and sometimes may be refound.

Notes. Nests on islands on both sides of the Baja peninsula. (For critical identification of *Synthliboramphus* murrelets and reference to the Oregon record, see Jehl and Bond [1975]. For details on a California breeding record on Santa Barbara Island, see Winnett et al. [1979].)

Ancient Murrelet

(Synthliboramphus antiquus)

Common some winters and scarce others; normal arrivals from the north do not appear in the California Pacific before October. The species builds in numbers during November and is present into early April. It is generally rare south of Monterey County. Ancient Murrelet is extremely rare anywhere in the California Pacific from May through September, but there are records for it in each month. Somewhat amazing is the fact that this Pacific Ocean species has been recorded in 4 Canadian provinces and 14 states that are landlocked. In June 1990, one turned up in northern England! In inland California there are two records for the Salton Sea and one for Palm Springs!

Identification. Unique in possession of several characteristics, this species is unmistakable, given a reasonable view. Its black crown, face, and chin (and in breeding plumage, throat) sharply contrast its light gray back. Its bright white underparts extend well up onto the neck, almost forming a white collar. The yellow bill is visible at a surprising distance.

Behavior. Ancient Murrelet is sometimes seen from points of land or beaches but also well offshore. Unlike other murrelet species that are almost always seen in twos (a pair or an adult with a chick) or ones, Ancients may be found in small flocks of up to 20 individuals (45 once at Southeast Farallon). In flight the sides of the body are narrowly but sharply black, contrasting with the white breast and belly and white underwing coverts, and the head is held higher than the body line. Other murrelets have more drawn out or flatter postures.

Notes. Nests in holes and crevices of rock piles in the Aleutians and other Alaskan islands, where most parental activity takes place at night. Two-day-old chicks leap into the sea, where they complete their growing period. They are accompanied by a single parent. Ancient Murrelets also are native to the nearshore Northwest Pacific, wintering south to Japan.

Cassin's Auklet
(Ptychoramphus aleuticus)

Common year-round in the California Pacific, but due to its far-flung foraging preference and nocturnal ways at nesting localities, it is commonly seen by one-day boats only from early September through January. An exception occurs at Cordell Bank, where, when upwellings erupt, many of the 47,000 breeding birds from Southeast Farallon forage. Cassin's Auklets may also be found west of the Farallones and west of the northern Channel Islands. In fall, birds from Canada and Alaska move in, and the species may be found in abundance at productive feeding areas such as Monterey, as well as many miles seaward over very deep water.

Identification. Small, like murrelets. Uniform medium-gray above, including throat and breast. Cassin's is definitely light-bellied (but this does not show on swimming birds and may be seen only with ventral flying views) but never gives the impression of a black-and-white bird, as do all murrelets in winter plumage. It is basically a tough, stubby little gray ball of feathers with white crescents above and below the eye. The whitish iris and base to the mandible are the only other bits of pattern.

Marbled Murrelet in summer plumage is similarly grayish brown but does not have an extensively whitish belly, has a *mot-*

Top: *Ancient Murrelet (p. 148). (Rich Stallcup)* Inset: *Cassin's Auklet (p. 149), running for take-off. (Rich Stallcup)* Bottom: *Cassin's Auklet. (Mark Rauzon)*

tled appearance, and in flight has more pointed wings. Cassin's wingtips appear more stiff and rounded than do those of all murrelets and of the larger Rhinoceros Auklet. The large Crested Auklet, very much a rarity here, is darker than Cassin's, especially on the crown and nape, has a pale bill, and is dark-bellied. On the water, all winter murrelets show a lot of white; Cassin's Auklet does not.

Although voice is of little use in identifying alcids at sea (because they seldom make any noise), it should be mentioned that most are quite vocal at breeding colonies. Field guides say that Cassin's Auklet's voice is "cricket-like chirping" or "weak croaking." These are not terms that anyone would use who has walked on Southeast Farallon at night during the breeding season. Several thousand birds may be calling at the same time, and the result is deafening. William Leon Dawson, in his classic *Birds of California*, related the place to a huge outdoor insane asylum with 100,000 little inmates screaming "Lemme outa here, lemme outa here" all at once.

Behavior. At sea, Cassin's Auklets are sometimes found in ones or twos, but at feeding spots (some of which shift around), hundreds or thousands are not unusual. Even where the species is abundant, it is not always easy to get a good look at one of these birds, as they are quite spooky. They pat-pat-patter directly away on foot to gain flight, unlike the ignited liftoff of murrelets, and take off very low. Ones too full to fly dive repeatedly and for long periods.

Parakeet Auklet
(Cyclorrhynchus psittacula)

Apparently common in the past, at least in some winters, south to Monterey Bay and probably beyond. Many of the 30 or so extant specimens were found dead or dying on beaches, but 14 birds collected on Monterey Bay between 13 and 30 January 1908 suggest that Parakeet Auklets were present in large numbers. The only recent onshore records are one (beached) at Moss Landing, Monterey County, in late January 1974 and another at the mouth of the Santa Maria River in the summer of 1988. The main winter range is unknown, but the North Pacific Gyre is a likely suspect. There are about 40 records, some of live birds, from the northwest Hawaiian Islands!

Parakeet Auklets may be regular off California in winter but beyond the range of one-day boat trips. On 8 December 1988, three were positively identified (two 95 miles west of Point Arena and one 78 miles west of Point Cabrillo), and five other alcids were said to be "almost certainly Parakeets." Another recent record is of an alternate-plumage bird 11 miles southwest of Point Año Nuevo, in San Mateo County, on 9 June 1989. The reliability of the observers is beyond question. Here is another case in which bigger and faster vessels, specifically sailing on overnight trips to study birds, will clear up questions of distribution.

Identification. A medium-sized auklet, Parakeet Auklet is blackish-gray above and entirely bright white below from the throat to the undertail coverts. In flight and on the water, it shows much more white on breast and sides than Cassin's or Rhinoceros auklets. The short, stout bill has a strongly recurved lower mandible, producing a nice smile. The bill is red or reddish-orange in summer and turns more dull pink or brown in winter. The iris is white, obvious on the dark face, and in combination with the strange bill and facial plume gives the bird a clown face. In flight, the neck is often extended and the bird looks around. In this way it resembles a small duck, whereas the other auklets are just footballs with wings. Because Parakeet Auklets acquire "summer" plumage in winter (the neck turns dark gray in front), most birds from California have had a red bill and the single, white, facial plume that extends back and down from the eye.

Behavior. On the water, this species resembles other medium-sized alcids in being not particularly skittish (as small alcids are), and it may allow reasonably close approach by boats, preferring to dive rather than fly. Though Parakeet Auklets do fly low over the water, their flight is often higher than that of other auklet species and more like that of puffins. Their habit of rolling from side to side in flight is not unique but may be helpful for seeing both dorsal and ventral features.

Notes. Two old records from Southern California, one at La Jolla on 28 January 1937 and one at San Simeon on 6 February 1955, may be acceptable, but since the birds were said to be "more or less decomposed" there is a possibility that their bodies drifted down from farther up the coast or from far at sea.

Crested Auklet

(Aethia cristatella)

Accidental. There is only one record for the California Pacific, that of a live beached bird at Bolinas, Marin County, on 16 July 1979 (found dead the next day). Another, apparently healthy, individual was seen on 7 July 1980 9 miles east-southeast of Cedros Island off Baja, 300 miles south of the U.S. border. It was said to be a "stunning adult in breeding plumage" and "whirred off, landing about 1 km. away." Though the latter record was certainly a surprise, in the Western Pacific the species winters south to Japan, so southerly occurrences on the eastern side may be expected. The only other record for the Eastern Pacific south of Alaska is from British Columbia. One was collected by a sealer off Vancouver in the winter of 1892–1893.

Identification. A medium-sized, all blackish-gray auklet, darker above than below, with a thick, stubby, reddish-orange bill, a yellow iris, and recurved "quail-like" feathers protruding from the forecrown. Like Parakeet Auklet, Crested has but one white facial plume, which flares back from the eye.

Crested is rather like other dark alcids (Cassin's and Rhinoceros auklets), but the spiked feather-crop on the forecrown distinguishes it from all but Whiskered Auklet, a smaller bird with more white facial plumes. Whiskered Auklet has not been found south of Alaska (Aleutian Islands) and Siberia. Only slightly bigger than a Cassin's Auklet, Crested is only two-thirds the size of a Rhinoceros Auklet. You will have to look each bird right in the face to see who it is.

Behavior. In Arctic waters, Cresteds are highly gregarious with others of their kind, plus Least and Parakeet auklets, so a healthy bird off California in winter might conceal itself within a flock of Cassin's or perhaps Rhinoceros auklets. A summer bird is more likely unhealthy or disoriented and may well be alone on the water. (The absence of other alcids at this season also supports this conclusion.)

Notes. Because the two California Pacific records are for summer, that may be the best time to look for nearshore Crested Auklets (as it is for Horned Puffins). Even if you don't connect with any rare alcids on your summer pelagic trip, at least you will see a lot of Black-footed Albatross — and the water is likely to be calm.

Top: *Parakeet Auklet (p. 151)*. *(Tom Schwan)* Inset: *Horned Puffin (p. 157), winter plumage. (Rich Stallcup)* Middle: *Rhinoceros Auklet (p. 156). (John Luther)* Bottom: *One Horned and three Tufted (p. 158) puffins. (Ed Greaves)*

Least Auklet
(Aethia pusilla)

Accidental. There is only one record for the California Pacific and for North America south of Kodiak Island, Alaska. The bird, an adult male, was found disabled on 15 June 1981 at Thornton State Beach, San Mateo County. It did not respond to care, died that night, and has become a resident in the skin collection at the Museum of Vertebrate Zoology, University of California at Berkeley. Note the date, and compare with records of Crested and Parakeet auklets and Horned Puffin!

Identification. Tiny and thick. Least Auklets are mostly dark grayish-brown above and white below but are spotted or marbled along the contact zone, giving them a molty look even when in fresh plumage. Other than the white throat, belly, and undertail coverts, they look mostly dark while sitting or swimming. In flight, the white scapular tips form "racing stripes" down the base of the wings. The dark bill may have an orange tip, and the iris is white. A single narrow white stripe flares back from mid-eye.

Cassin's Auklets are more extensively dark, being white only on the belly and lacking the white throat, "racing stripes," undertail coverts, and facial stripe. Cassin's bill is bluish to blackish, and these birds, though small, are noticeably larger than Leasts. Also consider Crested Auklet and Marbled Murrelet changing from summer to winter plumage.

Behavior. At sea, Least Auklets are skittish, like Cassin's Auklets, and when seen are often splat-splat-splattering away. In flocks, they sometimes form a ball instead of the line flight always performed by Cassin's and Rhinoceros auklets. Leasts' flight when startled may be erratic, rolling side to side, and the birds look around. This is true of all small auklets. Murrelets fly straight. Leasts are *tiny*, and even when seen quite well are often barely observed, slipping through a crack in the horizon.

Notes. Curiously, this species, like Crested Auklet, Horned Puffin, and perhaps Parakeet Auklet and Kittlitz's Murrelet, may be more productively searched for in the California Pacific from May into August than in winter, but records are yet too few at any season for serious generalization.

Rhinoceros Auklet

(Cerorhinca monocerata)

Common in late fall and early spring and occasionally abundant in winter. Like most alcids (except Craveri's and Xantus' murrelets), Rhinoceros Auklet is generally more common and widely distributed off Northern than Southern California. In winter, though, Rhinoceros Auklet is less common north than south of Sonoma County. (This statement is one of microgeography and refers only to this bit of the California Pacific.)

In 1974, just 5 years after Point Reyes Bird Observatory became steward of the Farallon Islands and removed a large population of European hares, Rhinoceros Auklets returned to nest there following an 80-year absence, and the current population is an estimated 250 pairs. The only suspected nesting for this species farther south is at Point Arguello, Santa Barbara County, where there may be 15 to 20 pairs. Recently, one bird was found in a burrow on Año Nuevo Island, San Mateo County. A few nest on outer Point Reyes and on rocks off Humboldt and Del Norte counties, California. The vast majority of the world population is north of California, all around the North Pacific, and south on the west side to Korea.

Identification. A large, dark puffin-like alcid with a whitish belly, which shows only in flight. High-plumage adults have two white plumes on the head, an orange bill with a white "rhino horn" at the base of the culmen (dorsal edge of the upper mandible), and a yellow iris. Winter adults are similar but lack the plumes. Juveniles are more blackish around the head, and many have thinner all-dark bills and dark irises.

Rhinoceros Auklets are larger and darker than Cassin's Auklet or murrelets, and young Tufted Puffins are the only real lookalikes. The puffin, a rarer bird, always has a bulbous bill that is deeper than any Rhinoceros Auklet's. Young puffins' bills may be dark or yellowish-orange, but they are thicker even than adult Rhinoceros Auklets' bills, and the puffin's head itself is bigger. On the water, the crown of any-age Tufted Puffin is high and blocky; that of Rhinoceros Auklet is flatter. In flight, Tufted Puffin has rounded wingtips and a dark belly, whereas the wingtips of Rhinoceros Auklet are more pointed and the belly is whitish.

Behavior. Rhinoceros Auklet is a pelagic species ranging quite far seaward, but it can be seen from shore. Winter dawn flights past Point Piños at the tip of the Monterey Peninsula can be impressive: 12,000 were estimated leaving Monterey Bay on 27 December 1974. While these are mostly distant fly-bys, the species may be seen more clearly from other coastal points. It sometimes occurs very near shore, in protected bays and, rarely, harbors. In summer, individuals may be seen near breeding rocks off Humboldt and Del Norte counties and from Point Reyes Lighthouse and Chimney Rock, Marin County. Getting on a boat makes close viewing much more likely.

Unlike Cassin's Auklet and murrelets, this species is often rather tame, allowing close approach by boats. Its dives may last up to two minutes.

Horned Puffin
(Fratercula corniculata)

Rare and not recorded every year in the nearshore California Pacific, but likely regular and perhaps common well beyond the continental shelf. Between 29 and 30 April 1989, 136 were counted 70 to 90 miles west of Point Reyes. When present nearshore, Horned Puffins are often widespread but not in large numbers. May and June are the best months off Southern California, and June and July off Northern California, suggesting that in some years Horned Puffins may winter south and maybe far west of California. (There are 3 records from the Northwest Hawaiian Islands.) Then, delayed somehow in their northward migration (perhaps because of a lack of flight feathers due to molt), some birds in early summer are moving slowly (swimming?) to the north. Most individuals found here are less than one year old, but healthy adults have been seen. In addition to this irregular summer occurrence, there is also a scattering of individual records from fall and midwinter, mostly in February and mostly of birds dead on beaches.

Much more common and widespread in the far North Pacific, including the Asian side. The species has been recorded breeding at Protection Island at the top of the Olympic Peninsula, Washington, has been seen on rocks off Oregon, and 1 landed on Southeast Farallon in June 1989! As we go to press, June 1990, at least 6 seemingly healthy Horned Puffins are sitting on the water at Chimney Rock, Point Reyes, Marin County, California!

Identification. Since Common Puffin *(F. arctica)* is *most* unlikely here, the crisp definition between the black upperparts and white underparts and the puffin bill will identify Horned Puffin.

Behavior. Like Tufted Puffin, Horned is usually found singly at sea, but during "invasion" periods several may be seen on one day. Though they may dive, puffins usually stay put and allow close approach by boats.

Tufted Puffin
(Fratercula cirrhata)

Currently only known to nest north of San Francisco, mostly on islands but also on steep headlands from Point Reyes north. Tufted Puffins formerly nested on the northern Channel Islands but mysteriously disappeared by the 1940s. A pair seen at Hurricane Point Rocks on 12 June 1980 was not confirmed as nesting, and none has been seen there since. On the Farallones, numbers remained very low until the early 1970s, when a large population of introduced European hares was entirely removed. Since then, numbers of puffins have risen from about 12 to about 40 pairs. Away from nesting spots, Tufted Puffins are scarcely seen, though there are scattered records throughout the year, some from Monterey, increasingly from north of there, and *exceptionally* from the south, even to waters off San Diego. The winter whereabouts of this species is not entirely understood, but far to sea or far north along the coast are good guesses.

Identification. Summer adults could not be mistaken for any other bird. Winter adults and, more so, juveniles could be mistaken for Rhinoceros Auklets. Both species are large, blackish alcids (Tufted Puffin is all black, Rhinoceros Auklet has a whitish belly not visible on swimming birds), and although Tufted Puffin always has a bigger and deeper bill, the difference between a large-billed Rhinoceros Auklet and a small-billed Tufted Puffin can be a close call under less than ideal circumstances. The domed crown of Tufted Puffin is clearly different from the flat-headed look of Rhinoceros Auklet. Horned Puffin, a late winter and summer rarity, is black above and sharply white below, the white being obvious even on swimming birds.

Behavior. Away from nests, Tufted Puffins are usually found singly. When found on the water, though they may dive, they usually stay put and allow close approach by boats. Unlike most alcids, Tufted Puffins may be attracted to feeding flocks at boats, especially if the boat is stopped.

Notes. Much more common and widespread in the far North Pacific, including the Asian side. This is true of all Pacific alcids except Craveri's and Xantus' murrelets and Cassin's Auklet.

Tufted Puffin (p. 158), winter adult. (Rich Stallcup)

Often in fall and seldom in spring, landbirds are seen on offshore trips. Many are disoriented nocturnal migrants that overflew the coast the previous night and are desperately trying to survive by finding shelter. The small passerines (perching birds) are tired and out of energy. They are attracted to boats (islands), usually circling and sometimes landing on mastings, railings, or people. Attempts to identify these birds should be made, as a fair percentage of them will be vagrants from the East with faulty compasses.

Since nocturnal migrant landbirds have been proven, at least in part, to navigate by the stars, periods of high overcast (and light breezes) cause more birds to make mistakes. Imagine the uncertainty a Chestnut-collared Longspur (a field bird of the Great Plains) must have felt circling a boat off Monterey or of a Cape May Warbler perched on a small dory far offshore Humboldt County. Some make safe landfalls on islands or the mainland, but many more drown or are overtaken and devoured by gulls and jaegers. Larger, stronger birds (herons, falcons, shorebirds, and owls) are also found at sea but are seldom attracted to boats and probably have better success rates at returning to safety on the mainland.

The landbirds seen from boats are, of course, but a fraction of those waifs that make the big error. Point Reyes Bird Observatory biologists on Southeast Farallon Island, a small granitic monolith 27 miles west of San Francisco, have recorded 375 species of birds (mostly misoriented migrants) and have seen waves of passerines numbering in the thousands.

Whales, Dolphins, and Porpoises

Cetaceans — whales, dolphins, and porpoises — have completely abandoned their terrestrial ancestral homes and, except for the need to breathe air, are now as aquatic as fish. They are intelligent and usually docile. They communicate by "speaking" to each other by name, can direct each other to specific actions, and have complex family and social behaviors. It is not unusual to find several species of cetaceans traveling or feeding in mixed groups.

There are two basic models, or suborders: **Mysticeti, the baleen whales,** feed mostly on krill sifted from huge mouthfuls of water through long, louvered curtains of baleen growing from the upper mandible. **Odontoceti, the toothed whales, dolphins, and porpoises,** feed on fish and squid (and, for Orca, sometimes other cetaceans, pinnipeds, and otters). They chase their prey and chomp onto it with sharp, paired teeth.

Right Whales. Family Balaenidae

Northern Right Whale
(Eubalaena glacialis)

Because of overkill by whaling interests in Alaskan waters in the late nineteenth century, Northern Right Whales were very nearly exterminated. Today, only a few hundred of these baleen whales remain in the entire North Pacific. Though Right Whales are occasionally seen in Alaskan waters and rarely south to Oregon, the tiny number of recent sightings (all March to May) in the California Pacific indicates that chances of seeing the species on a one-day trip (or hundreds of them) are dismal at best.

Right Whales are black or nearly so, have crusty bumps or bonnets in front of the dual blowholes, and exhale powerful V-shaped blows. There is no dorsal fin.

Top: *V-shaped blow of Bowhead Whale, shown here, is the same as that of Northern Right Whale (p. 161). (Larry Spear)* Middle: *Blue Whale (p. 163), baleen. (Dawn Breese and Bernie Tershy)* Bottom: *Blue Whale, nostrils. (Dawn Breese and Bernie Tershy)*

The common name has resulted from the fact that these slow-swimming large whales were the right ones to kill because they float after death. Bad luck for *Eubalaena*.

Rorqual Whales. Family Balaenopteridae

Blue Whale
(Balaenoptera musculus)

This baleen whale is the largest animal ever to live on Earth, with individuals in the Atlantic population exceeding 100 feet in length and weights of 150 tons. Those in the North Pacific reach *only* about 85 feet, with females larger than males of the same age. At close range, Blue Whales are entirely light blue-gray above, variously mottled with whitish. They are white to yellow below. Fin and Humpback whales are more blackish.

Blue whales exhale a massive columnar blow (like a decapitated fire hydrant) that can be seen at great distances. Only the blow of the Fin Whale approaches its height. Following the blow, the Blue Whale's massive back seems to roll on and on before the nub of a dorsal fin appears. Blues may stay submerged for 6 to 20 minutes after sounding. They frequently show flukes during deep dives or during shallow dives while traveling. Krill are virtually their only food. Usually found singly or in small herds of up to 5, as many as 40 Blues have been encountered feeding in certain special areas (Cordell Bank in fall 1987).

Following rigid protection throughout most of the world, Blue Whales have responded favorably, and the population is increasing. Although they are always a very special treat, sightings of these whales during summer and fall near the continental shelf are becoming almost a matter of routine.

Top: *Blue Whale (p. 163), forward part of the back. (Rich Stallcup)*
Middle: *Fin Whale (p. 165), dorsal fin (Ed Harper)* Bottom: *Fin Whale. (Ron LeValley)*

Fin Whale
(Balaenoptera physalus)

This baleen whale is also large (to 70 feet) and has a tall columnar blow similar to that of the Blue Whale. At close range, however, Fin Whales are charcoal-gray or black and lack pale mottling. The dorsal fin, located similarly on Fin and Blue whales (two-thirds of the way back), is relatively larger and more obvious. The flukes are rarely shown. Because the North Pacific population was savagely reduced by activities of whaling stations — even in California and even into the 1960s! — the Fin Whale is now rarely encountered nearshore. If we can keep the oceans clean and healthy, perhaps large pods will once again roam the offshore area in summer and fall. Most Fin Whales identified recently have been from southern Monterey County south, and well offshore.

Sei Whale
(Balaenoptera borealis)

A large (up to 65 feet), streamlined, fast (up to 20 knots) deep-water baleen whale, which, in part because of excessive hunting by the U.S. whaling industry as late as the 1960s, is seldom encountered in the California Pacific. Most similar to Fin Whales, Seis (rhymes with "bays") are dark gray to blackish above, but most have numerous egg-shaped white or gray spots. The dorsal fin is distinct — strongly recurved and (unless chewed) sharp. As with other baleen whales, this fin is located posteriorally but subtly farther forward than on Fin Whale and distinctly farther forward than on Blue Whale. As with Fin Whale, the blow of Sei is wide and rather flat on top, but it is not as bold or substantial as Fin's or Blue's. Like Blues, Sei Whales usually roam in pods of two to six individuals. The best hope of making their acquaintance in the nearshore Pacific is in late summer and early fall.

Top: *Minke Whale (p. 167). (Dawn Breese and Bernie Tershy)*
Middle: *Three Humpback Whales (p. 167), showing blow and flat back (rear), humped back during dive (left), and tail stock before flukes (right). (Thomas Jefferson/Intersea Research)* Bottom: *Breaching Humpback. (Thomas Jefferson/Intersea Research)*

Minke Whale
(Balaenoptera acutorostrata)

T his smallest of the northern baleen whales is relatively common in the nearshore Pacific, especially during autumn. In winter Minkes are frequently seen off Southern California and western Mexico. Their small size (to 35 feet for the larger females), indistinct exhalations, quick surface periods, and solitary nature make them much less obvious and less well known than their flamboyant larger cousins.

The sharp, falcate dorsal fin is located two-thirds to the rear, and because the animal is short, the fin may appear while the small blow is still settling. Minkes are dark gray to blackish above and white below. The most striking and singularly diagnostic feature is a bold white bar across the dark gray pectoral flipper. Though seldom seen by people on small, surface-level boats, this mark (when noted) will identify the animal. Often a large portion of the back and tail stock may be seen when the Minke begins a deep dive, but the flukes never clear the surface.

Occasionally Minke (rhymes with "pinky") Whales will approach boats to have a "look," but more often they scamper behind distant swells, as if trying to be difficult.

Humpback Whale
(Megaptera novaeangliae)

T hese baleen whales are well known as the "singing whales," and they have starred on several records, tapes, and TV shows. Their awesome leaps and breaches, which display their magnificent, winglike white flippers, have also deeply impressed whale visions into the minds of humans.

In the California Pacific, usually 1 to 5 Humpbacks travel together, but large pods of up to 60 animals may be seen anywhere offshore from spring through fall. Large numbers have shown up with recent (and perhaps historic) regularity between October and December at Cordell Bank in the Gulf of the Farallones National Marine Sanctuary. Though the population is slowly increasing, there may still be fewer than 1,000 in the entire North Pacific.

Humpbacks are large (up to 50 feet) and shining black, often with crustings of barnacles about the head and blowholes, which

Gray Whales (p. 169). Top: *exhaling*. *(Rod Norden)* Middle: *knuckles*. *(Thomas Jefferson)* Bottom: *face*. *(Ron LeValley)*

appear white. The long flippers are white, and the often-seen tail stock and flukes are black above. After the animal blows, its massive back mountains high above the water with the small, broad-based but nublike dorsal fin riding above. This humped back will identify the species at long range. The blow is dense but mushroom-shaped, not usually as towering as that of Blue and Fin whales. Dives may last more than 15 minutes.

Humpbacks are very athletic for large whales, and they perform multiple, sometimes tandem, breaching throughout the year. Lunge-feeding (power lunches) is another acrobatic behavior thrilling to see. The lunge in this case is forward, and only about half the body usually exits the water, powering the mouth into a krill swarm.

Many Humpbacks known as individuals by the distribution and pattern of black and white on the ventral flukes have been identified again and again at different places. Try for photos as they dive away — maybe your animal has a known history.

The Gray Whale. Family Eschrichtiidae

Gray Whale
(Eschrichtius robustus)

The Gray Whale is no doubt the most thoroughly known and popular marine mammal between southern Baja and Alaska. Its twice-annual nearshore migration and acrobatic outbursts have thrilled millions of terrestrial and aquatic whale watchers and have helped bring into focus the need for humanity to lovingly coexist with, and care for, marine mammals and the marine environment.

Adults are gray, are variously encrusted with patches of barnacles, and may reach lengths of slightly over 40 feet. The blow is fairly conspicuous but misty, and heart-shaped from the front or rear. There is no dorsal fin but rather a series of bumps, called knuckles, along the ridge of the tail stock; these are apparent as the animal rolls. The flukes are usually shown during dives.

Migrating Gray Whales normally travel in groups of 1 to 3, but sometimes pods of 15 or more are seen. With a population now estimated at 15,000, California Gray Whales are approaching numbers similar to estimated pre-whaling levels.

Sperm Whale
(Physeter macrocephalus)

T he model for Moby Dick, this is the largest toothed whale (up to 49 feet). Rarely seen nearshore, sperm whales are more at home over very deep water. They can dive to depths of well over a mile and remain submerged for more than an hour. Their primary food is squid, but numerous fish species, other pelagic life forms, and odd inanimate objects (rocks, a glass, a net float, someone's boot) have been identified from stomachs.

Sperm Whales (when found) are usually in large pods, but small groups and even single animals occur. Occasionally one will turn up in association with other large cetaceans. During the winter of 1988–1989, one was repeatedly seen by Whale Center cruises just west of the Farallones with a herd of Humpbacks.

Sperm Whales have huge, blocky heads that may involve up to 40% of the body length, and a single blowhole is mounted *far forward on the left.* The blow, projected forward at an angle, is rather short and dense. The brown to gray-brown body is dark. While resting on the smooth ocean surface, Sperm Whales resemble huge logs.

Pygmy Sperm Whale
(Kogia breviceps)
Dwarf Sperm Whale
(Kogia simus)

T hese two small toothed whales are very rare and, when seen, are most often stranded on beaches. When encountered at sea, they often remain just below the surface, allowing good views and easy identification, at least to genus. One (identified as *K. simus*) six miles northwest of Point Piños, Monterey Bay, did just that. There were eight- to ten-foot smooth, rolling swells, and we were idling parallel to the animal about 100 feet away. It just lay there, and someone asked if it was alive. I told them to watch carefully and they would see it

Top: *Sperm Whale (p. 170), facing left, showing back and dorsal curve. (Ed Greaves)* Middle: *Dwarf Sperm Whale (p. 170). (Dawn Breese and Bernie Tershy)* Bottom: *Baird's Beaked Whales (p. 172). (Gary Friedrichsen)*

smile. When we were in a trough, the animal was parallel to us, at eye level and close, inside a ridge of water. (I thought of those little scorpions in desert trinket shops, forever still in their blocks of clear lacquer.) I knew it was a *Kogia;* I knew what once-in-a-lifetime views we were having of this rare animal; and I knew I was quivering with excitement. Then a wave washed our deck, and the connection was lost.

These are small whales (up to 11 feet in *breviceps* and 9 feet in *simus*), blue-gray to charcoal above, and whitish below. They are stogie-shaped with blunt, sharklike heads, underslung jaws, and many sharp teeth. The dorsal fin on both species is obvious and stands alone, but it is larger relative to body size and centered near midbody on *simus* and relatively smaller and definitely closer to the flukes than the head on *breviceps*.

Beaked Whales. Family Ziphiidae

Baird's Beaked Whale
(Berardius bairdii)

This toothed whale is one of only two members of the large family Ziphiidae that may be seen and identified with any regularity in the California Pacific. Even so, Baird's are rare, generally shy animals, seldom found near shore. Luckily, they are large, with mature females (longer than the males) exceeding 36 feet. They are also gregarious and are usually found in pods of 2 to 20 animals. When seen on the surface at a distance (that's often all you get), they may be lying still, resembling logs, or splashing in a small area like a hot-tub party. Unluckily, they usually dive if a boat approaches within a quarter mile. They can remain submerged for up to 35 minutes, often resurfacing far from the original locality, and their low, puffy exhalations make visual relocation difficult, especially in rough water. Those we have seen have been distinctly brown, or tan, which is unusual in cetaceans. Their color plus their length, distinct dorsal fin (more than 65% to the rear), and bulbous melon head with long beak will aid identification. Summer and fall are the best seasons to hope to see *Berardius*. Although this species has been seen inside Monterey Bay and around the Channel Islands, its preferred habitats are in the deeper offshore zone, particularly around Pioneer Seamount.

Small Beaked Whales
(Genera *Ziphius* and *Mesoplodon*)

There is little doubt that this group of small toothed whales is the least known of any mammals on Earth. All are apparently citizens of deep ocean habitats (over 3,000 feet), have small world populations, and are cryptic (long dives of up to an hour and little or no blow) in behavior. Even when they are encountered and well seen, their similarities usually defy specific identification. Most of what is known of them comes from individuals or groups stranded on mainland or island beaches.

Cuvier's Beaked Whale *(Ziphius cavirostris)* is larger than the others and may reach a length of 23 feet. It may be identified at sea by its rusty brown body mottled whitish and its manila-colored head. Its wary attitude, however, usually prevents such a pleasure.

Five members of the mysterious genus *Mesoplodon* are known from the North Pacific, mostly from dead or dying animals on the beach. They are Hubbs' Beaked Whale *(M. carlhubbsi)*, Stejneger's Beaked Whale *(M. stejnegeri)*, Hector's Beaked Whale *(M. hectori)*, Blainville's Beaked Whale *(M. densirostris)*, and Ginkgo-toothed Beaked Whale *(M. ginkgodens)*. Large adults of *Mesoplodon* reach about 16 feet in length. There is a short, usually recurved dorsal fin positioned about two-thirds of the way down the back. All have but a single pair of teeth, but this is difficult to observe at sea (ahem). Squid and deep-water fishes are the diet. Small beaked whales usually travel in pairs or in pods of up to 15 individuals. If you are lucky enough to see any of these at sea, just forget about specific identification. Simply wish them well, and celebrate your good fortune.

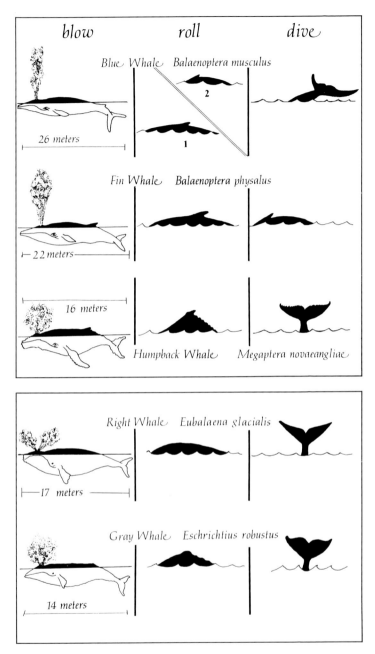

Comparison of blow, roll, and dive in large whales. Top: *Large whales with a dorsal fin: Blue (p. 163), Fin (p. 165), and Humpback (p. 167).* Bottom: *Large whales without a dorsal fin: Northern Right (p. 161) and Gray (p.169). (Ane Rovetta)*

False Killer Whale
(Pseudorca crassidens)

Rare in nearshore Northern California, the highly pelagic *Pseudorca* favors warmer waters to the south. Like other dolphins, *Pseudorca*s are gregarious and, when found, are usually in pods containing many individuals, often mixed with other small or medium-sized cetaceans, such as Bottlenosed or Risso's dolphins. For large animals (up to 18 feet), they can swim swiftly and, as they are often in "chorus lines," appear to scrimmage furiously along the water's surface. When feeling frisky, they are also exquisite acrobats.

Like Pilot Whale, *Pseudorca* comes only in basic black, but unlike Pilot Whale, *Pseudorca*'s long front end tapers banana-like to its mouth. Pilot Whales plow along creating a white-water wake with their blocky melon-heads. The more pointy *Pseudorca*s (though they sometimes do a lot of splashing) slice through waves. *Pseudorca*'s dorsal fin is much less broad-based than Pilot Whale's and is located more posteriorly.

Killer Whale
(Orcinus orca)

Actually the largest of the dolphins (adult males are at least 18 feet and eight tons), this magnificent black-and-white beast is known in friendlier terms simply as Orca. Nomadic predators, Orcas roam the sea searching for or following schools of large fish or pinnipeds. Groups are usually from 1 to 20 animals (a pod of about 60 at Cordell Bank, playing water polo with limp sea lions, was exceptional) and often contain males (with towering six-foot dorsal fins), females, and young. Although numbers have "incidentally" been killed through the years, no program specifically aimed at an Orca harvest has yet developed. Hallelujah! An ancestral home where many still persist is coastal northern Washington and southern British Columbia. This is the nearest area for us to make close personal contact with Orca. It is also where nearly 70 were captured in the 1960s

Top: *Orcas (Killer Whales) (p. 175). (Rich Stallcup)* Inset: *Cuvier's Beaked Whale (p. 173). (Bill Keener)* Middle: *Short-finned Pilot Whale (p. 177). (Ron LeValley)* Bottom: *Pseudorcas (False Killer Whales) (p. 175). (Gary Friedrichsen)*

and 1970s for theme parks and aquaria. More recently the capture source has switched to waters near Iceland, where Orcas are despised by some because they compete with commercial fishing interests.

Though June is the month of highest visitation at Southeast Farallon, Orcas may be seen in the California Pacific any time of year. Unfortunately their schedules are not available for human scrutiny, and their seasonal presence is mostly unpredictable. It is worth the wait, however, as encountering the big hunter in its realm is an entirely different adventure from watching one do tricks in the pond at the water world.

Short-finned Pilot Whale
(Globicephala macrorhynchus)

Although sometimes common off Southern California, these dolphins are definitely rare north of Point Conception. Adults may reach 16 to 18 feet in length, and the species travels in pods of up to several hundred animals, often in association with smaller cetaceans, particularly Bottlenose Dolphins. Pilot Whales are deliberate, rather slow swimmers and are easily (gently, now) approached by boats. They are mostly black with a shadowy gray saddle behind the dorsal fin. The dorsal fin itself, positioned well forward of midbody, is unusually broad-based and is wide, quite tall, and recurved. The strange dorsal fin, in combination with a large, round melon-head and depression at the blowhole, give the front end of the Pilot Whale a unique, lumpy look. In the California Pacific only the False Killer Whale could be a reasonable identification problem, but the latter has a more banana-shaped front end and a narrower dorsal fin perched closer to midbody.

Pacific White-sided Dolphin
(Lagenorhynchus obliquidens)

More conveniently called Lags, a reduction of their generic name, these lovely creatures are frequently encountered nearshore and offshore in fall, winter, and spring, especially during periods of warm water. They are very social, occurring in herds of from 20 to over 1,000 animals, often in company with other cetaceans, especially Risso's, Common, and Northern Right Whale dolphins. Fast-moving, highly acrobatic, and friendly, Lags are readily attracted to moving boats and often put on a splendid show. In June 1989, 5 Lags at the Pioneer Seamount were seen riding the bow wave of . . . a Humpback Whale.

Big Lags may be over seven feet long and are basically dark above and white below, with shining whitish sides. The dorsal fin is relatively large, broad-based, and strongly recurved. Its cutting edge and tip are black, while both sides of the "web" and trailing edge are white. The dorsal fin, quite different from those of Dall's and Harbor porpoises and from that of Common Dolphin (Northern Right Whale Dolphin doesn't have one), should identify the species.

Common Dolphin
(Delphinus delphis)

L ike the other dolphins of the California Pacific, Commons associate in large pods, sometimes of many hundred individuals. They are active and acrobatic swimmers, and sometimes several individuals may do tricks in tandem. Synchronized breathing, rolling, and diving (and probably feeding) behaviors are also sometimes exhibited.

The body's pattern is a complicated combination of blacks, whites, and grays, and individual variation exists, particularly on the dorsal fin. The behavior of the pod, shape of the dorsal fin (not as broad-based or as hooked as Pacific White-sided Dolphin's but larger and more recurved than Dall's or Harbor porpoise's), the cute little face, and the "beak" will identify the species.

The word *common* is a rather silly modifier to put before any animal's name. What is common in one place is rare or absent in others. Common Dolphin is common from Point Conception south into the tropics; uncommon from Point Conception north to Monterey (present only when the sea is warm); and hardly known north of there, where, if found, it should be called the "rare" dolphin. Two hundred seen off Southeast Farallon in September 1989 were at the limit of their range. Actually, *Delphinus delphis* lives in all the Earth's oceans, from tropical to

Top: *Pacific White-sided Dolphin (p. 177), (Rod Norden)* Middle: *Common Dolphin (p. 178). (Bill Keener)* Bottom: *Grampus (Risso's Dolphin) (p. 182), adult, with Rough-toothed Dolphins in background. (Dawn Breese and Bernie Tershy)*

warm temperate waters. Some populations have quite different appearances, and some have more descriptive, less ambiguous English names.

Bottlenose Dolphin
(Tursiops truncatus)

Because of the Bottlenose Dolphin's abundance in aquaria and theme parks, its worldwide distribution, the long-running television show *Flipper,* and its friendliness toward boats and human-related activities, it is probably the best known and most loved of all cetaceans.

In the California Pacific, *Tursiops* is common off the southern part of the state and distinctly rare north of the northernmost Channel Islands. In 1988, however, a small pod was seen body-surfing near the beach at Pacifica, just south of San Francisco.

Cetacean scientists have identified two distinct populations of *Tursiops,* one nearshore (along beaches, harbors, and bays), and the other living in deep water well offshore. In the nearshore population, groups are usually smaller, often fewer than ten, and offshore, groups often exceed twice that number. Apparently there is no way to physically identify any individual (except for *where* it is found), and it is not taxonomically clear what the population separation means. For now, just enjoy *Tursiops'* antics and friendliness. You'll hear about it if more than one species emerges.

Bottlenose Dolphins are large (to about 12 feet) and appear gray or brownish gray. They have a short and smiling beak and a broad, sharply recurved dorsal fin located midbody. They usually associate in small pods, but sometimes hundreds gather. They often associate with other cetacean species, such as Pilot and False Killer whales and Risso's and Pacific White-sided dolphins, but they also occasionally play with the big kids, such as Blue and Sperm whales. *Tursiops* are good acrobats and will come from some distance to race boats, ride the bow waves, and allow themselves to be tickled by vibrations caused by the propellers.

Top: *Northern Right Whale Dolphin (p. 182)*. *(Mike Danzenbaker)* Middle: *Northern Right Whale Dolphins in "chorus line." (Gary Friedrichsen)* Bottom: *Bottlenose Dolphin (p. 180)*. *(Ron LeValley)*

Risso's Dolphin
(Grampus griseus)

This large dolphin (up to 13 feet) is also commonly known by its generic name and just called Grampus or Gray Grampus. Though they may be found at any time of year, particularly during periods of warm water, there are more Grampus present, especially nearshore, in late summer and early fall. Though pods are often found in "albacore habitat," the relationship is probably circumstantial, since Grampus eat squid almost exclusively. Adult Grampus appear mostly whitish because of numerous scratches on the gray epidermis, most around the head and fewest on the pectoral and dorsal fins, leaving the latter areas darkest. The tall recurved dorsal fin, located midback, and the round whitish melon-head will identify the species. Grampus are easily approached and will ride the bow wave of large vessels but seldom approach small fishing boats. Highly gregarious, Risso's Dolphins may be found in homogeneous pods of up to several hundred individuals. They also party with other cetacean species: Pilot Whales, Bottlenose Dolphins, and Common Dolphins off Southern California; Pacific White-sided and Northern Right Whale dolphins off Northern California.

Because Grampus have not been the target of any major fishery, they should live long and prosper if we can clean up the Earth's oceans.

Northern Right Whale Dolphin
(Lissodelphis borealis)

When found, this superb, slender, shining, black-and-white dolphin is usually in very large pods and most often associating with other kinds of small cetaceans. Usually there are no Northern Right Whale Dolphins in sight, but when it rains it pours, and then they can be seen in all directions to the visual horizon. Synchronized swimmers, their running herds make low-angle leaps (dolphining), with sometimes hundreds of animals in "chorus line." They're there, then they're gone. They are very quick, perhaps able to swim 30 miles per hour for short periods, and they sometimes ride the bow wave of fast boats.

Right Whale Dolphins may be identified as far away as they can be seen. Often their large numbers will be an early hint, but their shiny blackness and lack of a dorsal fin are diagnostic features. Unlike any other North Pacific cetacean, the Right Whale Dolphin has a dorsal curve that is smooth and even, uninterrupted by barnacles, bumps, fins, or humps. They reach nine to ten feet in length but may give the impression of being much smaller. These animals are so fine and so active that the excitement one feels just being among them is as high the twentieth time as the first.

Restricted to the North Pacific (both sides) and partial to very deep water, they are seen most often nearshore between October and April. They become scarce south of Point Conception and, when present there, are usually far out to sea. The southern extreme of their range is off northernmost Baja California.

True Porpoises. Family Phocoenidae

Harbor Porpoise
(Phocoena phocoena)

A very small (five to six feet) porpoise that prefers inshore waters and is frequently seen from land. Shy and seemingly slow and determined when feeding, Harbor Porpoises are not attracted to boats or prone to acrobatic demonstrations. What they usually show is just a small brown or grayish back with a unique triangular dorsal fin at midbody. The activity usually observed is slow rolling. Harbor Porpoises are most often found singly, in pairs, or small groups, but hundreds may be found scattered at select shallow-water feeding areas, such as Drake's Bay, Marin County. Some are resident all year, but highest numbers are recorded in September and October. A cold-water species, Harbor Porpoise is rare south of Point Conception.

Because these animals are easily entangled in gill nets, the California population has recently been decimated, but this trend is reversible and, in fact, is being reversed.

Top: *Harbor Porpoise (p. 183)*. *(Ron LeValley)* Middle: *Dall's Porpoise (p. 185), showing "rooster tail." (Gary Friedrichsen)* Bottom: *Common Dolphin (p. 178)*. *(Ron LeValley)*

Dall's Porpoise

(Phocoenoides dalli)

This fine little (up to seven feet) black-and-white porpoise is frequently seen year-round in the California Pacific but, being a cold-water species, is more common north than south. Dall's are most often found in small herds. Unless feeding, these animals are readily attracted to boats and may ride the bow wave for several minutes. When feeding, Dall's are slow rollers that show an obvious hump at the base of the caudal vertebrae. When "running," they are extremely fast and typically splash a distinctive "rooster tail" of white water at each surfacing.

Dall's Porpoise. (Dan Taylor)

Sea Otter
(Enhydra lutris)

Though usually inhabiting kelp beds that are held fast to coastal rocks or islands, Sea Otters are *truly* marine mammals. All their life functions are carried out in the water, and healthy unstressed animals rarely if ever "haul out" on rocks, breakwaters, or beaches. Sea Otters are members of the family Mustelidae and are more closely related to weasels and skunks than to seals and sea lions. Lacking a layer of blubber, which all pinnipeds and cetaceans possess, Sea Otters are kept warm by their heavy fur coats, thickest of all animals' at 20,000 long hairs per square inch of skin. Their soft, luxuriant pelts were practically their demise.

Until well into the eighteenth century, Sea Otters were common and ranged throughout the North Pacific crescent from Baja up the coast through the Aleutians, the Komandorskiyes, the Kamchatka Peninsula, and the Kuril Islands to Japan. After their discovery as a valuable "resource," they were mercilessly persecuted, especially by the Russians, to near extinction. Hundreds of thousands were slaughtered in the Aleutians and adjacent Siberia alone, and while a very few escaped detection there, the species was completely eliminated from Southeast Alaska south to California. In 1938, a small group of Sea Otters was rediscovered in the giant kelp forest off southern Monterey County. Through protection beginning early this century, the Alaskan population is strong and healthy, but along California there remain only about 2,000 individuals, most living on the Monterey shore. A single, poorly placed oil spill there or off southern Santa Cruz County could kill all of them.

Occasional otter sightings along the California coast north of San Francisco lend hope that some rehabitation might take place. At Southeast Farallon Island, where Sea Otters formerly occurred, there were no records in the twentieth century until one otter was seen at North Landing from 24 to 28 October 1986. This event was encouraging, but there have been no further observations during daily surveillance.

Best places to watch these wonderfully silly little guys are at Point Lobos, along the Seventeen Mile Drive through Pebble Beach, and along the Pacific Grove shore from Point Piños to Monterey Harbor.

Sea Otter (p. 186). (Mark Rauzon)

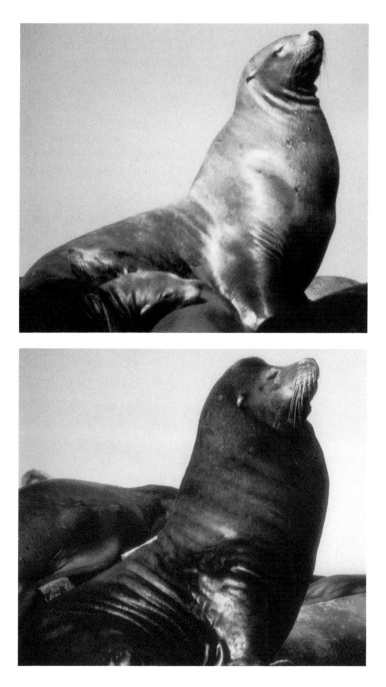

Male sea lions. Top: *Northern (Steller's) (p. 189).* Bottom: *California (p. 190). (Ed Harper)*

Seals and Sea Lions

Pinnipeds — or seals and sea lions — are amphibious marine mammals that spend large portions of their lives both at sea and hauled out on islands, beaches, and coastal rocks. While appearing friendly and even comical, they are effective predators, taking large numbers of fish, squid, and other aquatic invertebrates. Pinnipeds are not exactly loved by most anglers, but, like all marine mammals, they are now entirely protected in the near-shore Pacific.

Eared Seals. Family Otariidae

Northern (Steller's) Sea Lion
(Eumetopias jubatus)

More northerly and not as common as California Sea Lions in the California Pacific, Northern formerly boasted a population of at least 4,000 in the state, mostly north of Monterey. Adult males are easy to identify by their size (to ten feet and 2,000 pounds — 30% bigger than adult male Californias). Northerns have more pugged noses, shorter ear flaps, and more massive front flippers than Californias do, and a charming, very loud "roar" as opposed to California's "bark." In general, Northerns are a more pallid, sandy color than Californias, but all sea lions are darker wet than dry. Females and immatures are harder to identify, but the front flippers and voice should give them away.

Populations, including those on Southeast Farallon, drastically declined during the 1980s, perhaps due to a combination of toxins in the water (causing stillbirth) and increased disturbance by dive boats. Northern Sea Lion was listed for special concern as *threatened* in April 1990.

Some good places to still see hauled-out Northerns are at the Santa Cruz Lighthouse, Año Nuevo Point, Bird Rock off San

Francisco, Southeast Farallon, Bodega Rock off Bodega Head, and (in increasing numbers) to the north. (Remember, California Sea Lion is vastly more common along the California coast.)

California Sea Lion
(Zalophus californianus)

Clearly our most abundant pinnipeds, California Sea Lions may be seen (and heard!) year-round along rocky shores, breakwaters, harbors, rivermouths, islands, and the open sea. Their range spreads from southern British Columbia to mainland western Mexico and adjacent islands, with the center of abundance from San Francisco to islands off Baja California. Breeding happens only on the Farallones (rarely) and from the Channel Islands south.

The long pectoral flippers and external ear flaps typical of *Zalophus* are traits shared only by fur seals and Northern Sea Lions. Some caution must be used when identifying the rarer animals. Fur seals of both sorts are cuter, smaller, and have relatively longer whiskers. Male Californias may reach a length of seven and a half feet and a weight of 715 pounds. Northern Sea Lion, a cold-water animal that broadly overlaps the range of *Zalophus* from Point Conception north, is (given the same age and gender) a much larger, hunkier beast. Even young female Northerns, which are slightly more pug-nosed than *Zalophus*, are 30% bigger than their female cousins, have larger heads, smaller ear flaps, and much broader front flippers. Though male Northerns may be told from the darker brown *Zalophus* by their sandy pelage, coloration of sea lions is tricky, and wet ones are always darker than dry ones.

California Sea Lions have learned to follow fishing boats and will steal a lot of fish, but are entirely protected, and any attempt to harm one should be promptly reported to the local office of the California Department of Fish and Game.

Guadalupe Fur Seal
(Arctocephalus townsendi)

This smallest of the eared seals (sea lions) was pounded by human furriers in the late nineteenth and early twentieth centuries until the 1920s, when it was thought to be extinct. In 1954, 14 individuals were rediscovered on Guadalupe Island, and today the population may be more than 1,000 individuals. A few animals are now sometimes seen near historical rookeries at San Miguel and San Nicolas islands in the Channels. With great cosmic luck, perhaps breeding will be reestablished there. A small animal (males to six feet and 350 pounds), this fur seal's long muzzle (nose and foreface) is saddled or dorsally dented, which should distinguish adult Guadalupes from Alaska fur seals and from our two larger sea lions. Unaccompanied juveniles would be more difficult to identify.

Northern (Alaska) Fur Seal
(Callorhinus ursinus)

Much smaller (males to seven feet and 600 pounds) than sea lions of equal age and sex, and larger and more blunt-nosed than Guadalupe Fur Seals, Northern Fur Seals are easy to identify at sea. The short muzzle (the female's crown is convexly rounded between the nose and a point above the eyes), long dense whiskers, long external ear

Northern (Alaska) Fur Seal. (Gary Friedrichsen)

Ocean Birds

flaps, and sometimes the behavior will help. Often when a fur seal is encountered at sea, it will be floating buoyantly with one very long pectoral flipper overlapping the tip of one or both tail flippers, forming a canopy perhaps to shade and cool its body while it sleeps. The first time this configuration is seen, it appears to be a most inanimate object. When a boat gets close enough to waken the animal, the seal usually delivers an indignant stare before its splashing dive but will pop up to the surface for two or three more looks before final departure.

The world population of Northern Fur Seals is thought to be over 2 million, having recovered from an estimated low of 125,000 in 1911 when the Fur Seal Treaty became law. Today, bachelor bulls are scientifically "harvested" for their fur by Aleuts in the Pribilof Islands, Alaska, without threatening the healthy population numbers. A recently established (or reestablished) breeding colony on San Miguel in the Channel Islands represents a major range expansion. Formerly 80,000 bred on the Farallones but were wiped out there by Russians in the early 1800s. Now only an occasional male hauls out for a look and a wonder.

True Seals. Family Phocidae

Harbor Seal
(Phoca vitulina)

The Harbor Seal is basically an onshore pinniped seldom seen on the open sea. It does, however, occur, breed, and commute to and from offshore islands, such as the Farallones and the Channel Islands. Telemetry studies have shown long-range travel along the mainland coast. Being true seals, these animals have huge eyes and small pectoral fins (rather useless for mobility on land), and they lack the external ear flaps typical of sea lions and fur seals. Most of their fish-foraging likely occurs at night and up to several miles from landfall. Harbor Seals regularly enter bays, harbors, and river mouths. When departing the water's surface, they sink (like Elephant Seals) rather than leap-dive (like the eared seals).

Harbor Seals come in a wide variety of pelages (a furry way of saying plumages), from nearly black to nearly white or rusty, always with spots or ringlets of interruption.

Top: *Harbor Seal. (p. 192). (Leroy Jensen)* Bottom: *Northern Elephant Seals (p. 194). (Jules Evens)*

Northern Elephant Seal

(Mirounga angustirostris)

Virtually exterminated by hunters (and, in the end, zealous scientific collectors) in the late 1800s, the now protected Elephant Seal has recolonized most of its former range — a true environmental success story. Huge winter rookeries at Año Nuevo and on Southeast Farallon Island off San Francisco, near the northern border of the species' breeding range, bellow loudly of triumphant recovery. Thirty years ago there was dead silence.

Though highly pelagic when not at rookeries, Elephant Seals are seldom seen at sea. When seen, they are shy and (unlike eared seals) are not easily approached by boats. When resting, the Elephant Seal hangs vertically in the water with perhaps its anterior quarter nosing skyward above the surface. Because big bulls (from 15 to 18 feet long and 3,600 to 5,400 pounds) have such massive heads and "noses," they may be seen and identified at great distances. When one is spotted, take your distant looks, because the animal will sink before the boat gets a quarter mile from it. Unlike sea lions and fur seals, *Mirounga* will probably not reappear for a curtain call or second look.

Very deep divers, Elephant Seals eat bony and cartilaginous fishes as well as squid and, in turn, are often chewed upon by Great White Sharks or Orcas.

Sea Turtles

With low, sleek shells and legs that have evolved into huge, strong flippers, these large turtles are well adapted for life in the ocean. Except for laying eggs on beaches, they live entirely at sea. Because sea turtles are tropical by nature, the cold California Current keeps most species south of our region, but four are regular as far north as the Channel Islands off Southern California, and a fifth is, or was, rare. Strong swimmers, turtles are subject to long-distance vagrancy, and individuals often turn up far from their supposed range.

All California pelagic sightings should be reported with as much detail as can be gathered (precise locality, species, date and time, size of animal, and, if possible, water temperature). In addition to these details, any photographs available should be sent to your closest oceanographic research institute or major natural history museum.

All beached sea turtles should be documented by description and photographs. Promptly report their presence to state and federal wildlife agencies, local park rangers, and/or the curator of reptiles at the nearest natural history museum. Do not remove sea turtles even if they are dead. It is illegal for anyone except officials with permits to touch these animals.

The most obvious and diagnostic identification characteristics are color, overall shape, distribution of plates on the head, and the number of shields along the sides of the shell. For further help in identification of young turtles, see *A Field Guide to Western Reptiles and Amphibians* (Stebbins, 1985).

All sea turtle species are rare at best, and many populations are endangered or already extinct. Endless persecution throughout the turtle world for human food and tourist trinkets has severely punished these gentle citizens of the sea. Please support sea turtle conservation and passionately discourage the purchase or possession of turtle products.

Leatherback

Green Turtle

Pacific Ridley

Loggerhead

Sea turtles and top silhouettes. Top to bottom: Leatherback (p. 202), Green (p. 198), Pacific Ridley (p. 198), Loggerhead (p. 200). (Ane Rovetta)

Sea turtles: shell shape and plate count, dorsal view. Leatherback (p. 202), Green (p. 198), Loggerhead (p. 200), Pacific Ridley (p. 198). (Ane Rovetta)

Green Turtle
(Chelonia mydas)

Occasionally found off southernmost California, especially in waters from Los Angeles south. Extralimital animals have been recorded up the coast to British Columbia and even as far north as Admiralty Island, Alaska. The species may be expected anywhere along the California Pacific near the coast or well seaward over deep water. There is a recent northerly record from 2 September 1989 at Southeast Farallon Island.

Identification. Length to five feet. The shell is greenish or brownish to grayish-black (not much help), with four costal shields on each side, the anterior pair not meeting the nuchal shield. Head plates are distinctive, large and dark, and clearly but narrowly edged with yellow or cream. There is one especially large pair between the eyes. For memory, Green Turtle may be thought of as the one wearing a hair net (much better than a gill net). The whole shell is wide and low, with no overlapping shields.

Notes. A *threatened* species widely killed for its flesh as food and for its shell for tourist trinkets. This, plus the relentless harvesting of its eggs from nesting beaches, has contributed to its demise throughout its world range.

Pacific Ridley
(Lepidochelys olivacea)

Rarely seen, the Pacific Ridley has been recorded at Monterey and Mendocino and as far north as Humboldt County in Northern California.

Identification. The shell is dull greenish, with five or six to nine costal shields (usually more than any other sea turtle) on each side, the anterior pair bordering on the nuchal shield. The head is often very pale, with two pairs of large plates above the eyes. Smaller than other sea turtles, adults seldom reach three feet in length. The shell is flat, especially compared to that of the Loggerhead, and seen from above, its shape is more round than shells of the others.

Notes. Like Green and Loggerhead turtles, the Pacific Ridley is *threatened* because of human exploitation.

Top: *Green Turtle (p. 198). (Ron LeValley)* Bottom: *Pacific Ridley (p. 198). (Bill Keener)*

Loggerhead Turtle

(Caretta caretta)

Occasionally present in waters off Southern California, regularly north to San Luis Obispo County. Loggerheads are rare farther north, but the species has been recorded as far up the coast as southern Washington State. Occasionally seen near or east of the Channel Islands, Loggerheads may also be found on the open sea.

Identification. Length to seven feet. The shell of the adult is ruddy brown to quite reddish, with five or more costal shields on each side, the anterior pair bordering on the nuchal shield. Head plates are usually yellowish-olive with margins that are relatively uncontrasting, and the *lips are yellow*. The shell of adults is smooth, without shingled shields, and is distinctly high in front, steeply sloping to the rear. Young Loggerheads may have overlapping shields, three front-to-rear dorsal ridges like a Hawksbill Turtle, and a dull yellowish coloration to the shell.

Notes. Like Green and Ridley turtles, the continued existence of Loggerhead Turtle is *threatened* by human over-exploitation.

Hawksbill Turtle

(Eretmochelys imbricata)

Like Pacific Ridley, this is a small sea turtle that reaches only about three feet in length. By far the rarest of the five species recorded in the nearshore Pacific, it may be permanently extirpated here and in other large pieces of its historic range.

Identification. The shell is dark brown or greenish brown with paler yellowish or greenish marbling. It has a high, bony dorsal ridge, partly toothed, and each shield overshingles the one behind it. There are four costal shields on each side, and the anterior pair does not meet the nuchal shield. Cautiously now, remember that young Loggerheads may be dull yellowish, a bit marbled, and may have overlapping shields on a low dorsal ridge.

Notes. Hawksbill is officially considered *endangered* due to overharvesting by humans for its eggs, meat, and lovely patterned "tortoiseshell."

Top: *Loggerhead Turtle (p. 200). (Bernie Tershy and Craig Strong)*
Bottom: *Leatherback Turtle (p.202). (Ned Harris)*

Leatherback Turtle
(Dermochelys coriacea)

P robably the most widespread and often seen sea turtle in the nearshore Pacific, Leatherbacks have been found all along the California coast, and individuals have reached Alaska.

Identification. The shell is unique, without shields. Rather, as the species' name suggests, the shell has an overall leathery appearance, with five ridges, front to back, and valleys in between. The shell of most individuals is brown, some light and some dark. By far the largest extant turtles, Leatherbacks may reach eight feet in length and weigh almost a ton. Probably the most often seen turtle in the California Pacific, this is also the easiest to identify. In addition to the distinctive shell, the head and flippers lack large scales or plates and are very uniform.

One of Leatherback's favorite foods here is large jellyfish, and often the turtle's head may be inside one, wearing it like a helmet.

Notes. Of the five species of sea turtles recorded in the California Pacific, this is the only one with a surviving population large enough to have avoided dismal agency classification.

Yellow-bellied Sea Snake
(Pelamis platurus)

A true snake that is completely adapted for ocean habitats, *Pelamis* is virtually immobile on land. It is quite poisonous to its fish prey, which are quickly stunned when it bites. Human fatalities due to sea snake bites are very few, though, as this animal is shy rather than aggressive.

The snake's tail tip is laterally compressed into a very functional rudder. The nostrils are located high on the head and are closable. Ventral "scuts," highly adapted scales used for locomotion in terrestrial snakes, are absent.

Pelamis inhabits warm waters throughout the Indian and Pacific oceans and barely reaches California. It is rare as far north as waters off Orange County. It might be seen along slick lines where there are bubbles and flotsam, at kelp "paddies," or swimming eel-like in open water. Being a reptile, *Pelamis* needs to breathe air.

The Yellow-bellied Sea Snake is truly that. The entire dorsum is blackish, and the black above and yellow below are sharply demarked on the sides. The oarlike tail may be bright yellow with black markings, creating a stunning pattern.

Pelagic Red Crab
(Pleuroncodes planipes)

Pelagic Red Crabs are nomadic crustaceans that swim, drift, and flow around the Eastern Pacific from Panama north to Northern California. When present, their huge numbers cause the water to turn red, and when found, they are devoured by some baleen whales, pinnipeds, and some bird groups, such as tubenoses, gulls, terns, and alcids.

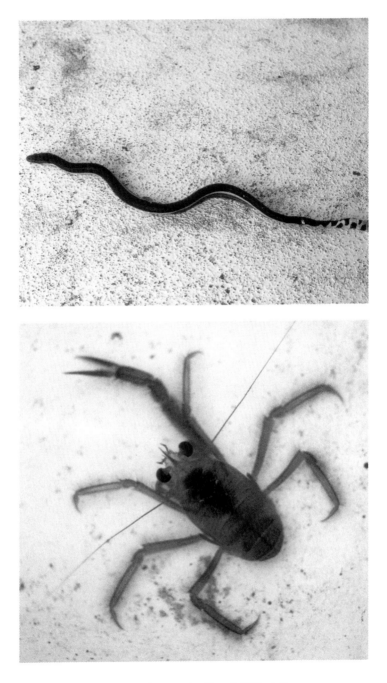

Top: *Yellow-bellied Sea Snake (p. 203). (Ron LeValley)* Bottom:
Pelagic Red Crab (p. 203). (Tom Johnson)

Pacific Ocean Sunfish

(Mola mola)

T his outrageous creature is the only member of the head-
fish family (Molidae) regularly seen off our West Coast.
Though more common to the south, it occurs into Alaskan waters, and numbers fluctuate throughout its range. Most
usual are two- to four-foot-long animals, but they may reach ten
feet and weigh 2,000 pounds!

When present, sunfish are often seen lounging at the surface.
They are white or pinkish, easily seen, and may be approached
very closely by boats. Gulls or fulmars are often in close atten-
dance, perhaps in hopes of snapping off some nice, juicy parasite.

Although hunted by some cultures and considered a delicacy
by others, the species is not the object of any Northeast Pacific
fishery. Sunfish are laterally compressed (like an angel fish at the
pet store), have a beaklike mouth, an eye on each side of the
head, and a fin on both the top and bottom of the back end.
They lie flat on the surface and are very friendly, usually waving
at passing boats.

Rock Cod

(Genus Sebastes)

R ock Cod (or Rock Fish) of the genus *Sebastes* are one
of several key links in the chain of life of the nearshore
Pacific. There are a lot of species (over 35 in Monterey
Bay alone), and some are abundant enough to support a large
human fishery. Since they do live in rocky areas of the sea, upwellings lift tons of their juveniles, eggs, and dead towards the surface.
Mixed with zooplankton and photoplankton, they form the nutri-
tious krill that is feasted upon by baleen whales and many birds,
especially terns and alcids.

Top: *Rock Cod (p. 205). (Jane Orbuch)* Middle: *California Flying Fish (p. 207), leaving "tracks" on the water. (Peter Pyle)* Bottom: *Blue Shark (p. 207).(John Luther)*

California Flying Fish

(Cypselurus californicus)

Because of its greatly enlarged, winglike pectoral fins, this animal is able to escape subsurface predators (such as various tuna) by swimming quickly and hurtling itself into the air for perhaps 50 yards. As it begins to slow down, the ventral web of the caudal fin is often dipped into the water, wiggled wildly, and the animal is again launched for possibly 30 more yards. Flying fish here are beautifully blue above and shining silver-white below.

This species of flying fish usually occurs from Point Conception south to and beyond Los Cabos, Baja Sur.

Blue Shark

(Prionace glauca)

The most often seen shark in nearshore California waters, more common to the south but also at times abundant in Monterey Bay and off Point Reyes. The caudal fin is practically the same size and shape as the exposed first dorsal fin, so that two "dorsal" fins are seen, one closely following the other. The first dorsal fin is closer to the pelvic fins than to the pectoral fins.

Individuals seen off California are mostly 3 to 7 feet in length, but in warmer, more tropical waters, they may reach 12 feet. Though not considered "man-eaters" here, they are aggressive feeders, and it is probably best to stay on the boat when Blue Sharks are present.

This may be the world's most migratory shark, with an individual known to have traveled between New England and Brazil. Blue Sharks travel in groups of the same gender, and they eat fish and squid. Though often seen nearshore, they are truly pelagic and are seldom found in water as shallow as 100 feet.

Prolific reproducers, Blue Sharks are known to have litters of 130 young!

Great White Shark
(Carcharodon carcharias)

Great White Sharks are not likely to be seen on one-day nature trips to sea except, perhaps, by some lucky (or unlucky) group near the Farallones in fall or winter. Because seals and sea lions are now protected and have made excellent population recoveries, islands and bits of the coast that support pinniped rookeries provide the conditions necessary for Great White Shark presence. The shark pictured here, eating a young elephant seal, was photographed from a Boston Whaler by Point Reyes Bird Observatory biologists studying the magnificent beast and its predation on mammals in the nearshore Pacific.

Great White Shark. (Peter Pyle)

Bibliography

Following is a selection of publications used in preparing this book or that might be useful to the reader.

I particularly want to recommend three outstanding books: for identification of ocean birds, Peter Harrison, *A Field Guide to Seabirds of the World* (1987); for becoming one with the moods of the nearshore Pacific and getting the real story of high times and horrors in the commercial fishing industry, *Neptune's Apprentice*, by Marie De Santis (1984); and for understanding issues and items affecting the coast, *California Currents*, by Marie De Santis (1985).

AINLEY, DAVID G. The occurrence of seabirds in the coastal region of California. *Western Birds* 7, no. 2.

AINLEY, DAVID G., AND B. MANOLIS. Occurrence and distribution of the Mottled Petrel. *Western Birds* 10, no. 3.

ALEXANDER, W. B. 1954. *Birds of the Ocean.* New York: Putnam.

AMERICAN ORNITHOLOGISTS' UNION. 1957. *Check-List of North American Birds.* 5th ed. Baltimore: A.O.U.

———. 1983. *Check-List of North American Birds.* 6th ed. Baltimore: A.O.U.

BERGER, A. 1981. *Hawaiian Birdlife.* 2d ed. Honolulu: University of Hawaii Press.

BEVIER, L. In press. Eleventh report of the California Bird Records Committee. *Western Birds.*

BLAKERS, M., S. DAVIES, AND P. REILLY. 1984. *The Atlas of Australian Birds.* Carlton, Australia: Melbourne University Press.

BROWER, K., AND W. R. CURTSINGER. 1979. *Wake of the Whale.* New York: Friends of the Earth.

BURT, WILLIAM H., AND RICHARD P. GROSSENHEIDER. 1976. *A Field Guide to the Mammals of America North of Mexico.* Boston: Houghton Mifflin.

DAWSON, WILLIAM L. 1923. *The Birds of California.* San Diego: South Moulton.

DE SANTIS, MARIE. 1984. *Neptune's Apprentice.* Novato, Calif.: Presidio Press.

———. 1985. *California Currents.* Novato, Calif.: Presidio Press.

DEVILLERS, P. The skuas of the North American Pacific Coast. *Auk* 94:417–429.

EVERETT, WILLIAM T. Biology of the Black-vented Shearwater. *Western Birds*, 9, no. 3.

FITCH, JOHN E., AND ROBERT J. LAVENBERG. 1971. *California Marine Food and Game Fishes.* Berkeley and Los Angeles: University of California Press.

FLINT, V. E., R. L. BOEHME, Y. V. KOSTIN, AND A. A. KUZNETSOV. 1984. *A Field Guide to Birds of the U.S.S.R.* Translated by Natalia Bourso-Leland. Princeton, N.J.: Princeton University Press.

GALLAGHER, M., AND M. WOODCOCK. 1980. *The Birds of Oman*. London: Quartet.

GARRETT, K., AND J. DUNN. 1981. *The Birds of Southern California*. Los Angeles: Los Angeles Audubon Society.

GASKIN, D. E. 1982. *The Ecology of Whales and Dolphins*. Exeter, Calif.: Heinemann Educational Books.

GRANT, P. J. 1982. *Gulls: A Guide to Identification*. 2d ed. Calton, England: T & A D Poyser Ltd.

HALEY, DAUPHINE, ed. 1984. *Seabirds of the Eastern North Pacific and Arctic Waters*. Seattle: Pacific Search Press.

———. 1986. *Marine Mammals of the Eastern North Pacific and Arctic Waters*. Seattle: Pacific Search Press.

HARRISON, P. 1983. *Seabirds: An Identification Guide*. Boston: Houghton Mifflin.

———. 1987. *A Field Guide to Seabirds of the World*. London: Christopher Helm.

HASEGAWA, H. 1978. The Laysan Albatross breeding in the Ogasawara Islands. *Pacific Seabird Group Bulletin* 5:16–17.

HUBBS, C. L. 1960. The marine vertebrates of the outer coast. In Symposium on the biogeography of Baja California and adjacent seas. Part II. *Marine Biotas. Syst. Zool.* 9: 134–147.

JEHL, JOSEPH R., JR. 1973. Late autumn observations of pelagic birds off southern California. *Western Birds* 4(2): 45.

———. 1982. The biology and taxonomy of Townsend's Shearwater. *Le Gergaut* 72:121–135.

JEHL, JOSEPH R., JR., AND S. I. BOND. 1975. Morphological variation and species limits of the genus *Endomychura*. *Transactions San Diego Society of Natural History* 18(2): 9–24.

JEHL, JOSEPH R., JR., AND K. PARKES. 1982. The status of the avifauna of the Revillagigedo Islands, Mexico. *Wilson Bull.* 94:1–19.

JOUANIN, C., AND J. MOUGIN. 1979. Procellariiformes. In Mayr, E. and G. W. Cottrell, eds. *Peter's Check-List of Birds of the World*. Cambridge, Mass.: Museum of Comparative Zoology.

KAZA, STEPHANIE. 1987. Return of the Elephant Seal. *Point Reyes Bird Observatory Newsletter* 76:1–4.

KING, W. 1974. *Pelagic Studies of Seabirds in the Central and Eastern Pacific*. Smithsonian Contributions to Zoology 158. Washington, D.C.

KNYSTAUTAS, ALGIRDAS. 1987. *The Natural History of the U.S.S.R.* New York: McGraw-Hill.

LEATHERWOOD, S., AND R. R. REEVES. 1983. *The Sierra Club Handbook of Whales and Dolphins*. San Francisco: Sierra Club Books.

LEATHERWOOD, S., R. R. REEVES, W. F. PERRIN, AND W. E. EVANS. 1982. *Whales, Dolphins and Porpoises of the Eastern North Pacific and Adjacent Arctic Waters*. NOAA Technical Report NMFS Circular 444.

LINDSEY, TERENCE R. 1986. *The Seabirds of Australia*. Sydney, Australia: Angus and Robertson.

LOOMIS, L. 1918. A review of the albatrosses, petrels and diving petrels. *Proceedings California Academy of Sciences, Series 4*, 2:1–187.

MCCASKIE, G., P. DEBENEDICTIS, R. ERICKSON, AND J. MORLAN. 1988. *Birds of Northern California*. Rev. ed. Berkeley: Golden Gate Audubon Society.

MCINTYRE, J. 1974. *Mind in the Water*. Covelo, Calif.: Project Jonah and Yolla Bolly Press.

MATTHEWS, L. H. 1978. *The Natural History of the Whale*. London: Weidenfield & Nicolson.

MILLER, T. 1975. *The World of the California Gray Whale*. Santa Ana, Calif.: Baja Trail Publications.

MURPHY, R. C. 1951. The populations of the Wedge-tailed Shearwater *(Puffinus pacificus)*. *American Museum* 1512 (November): 1–21.

———. 1958. *The Vertebrates of SCOPE, November 7– December 16, 1956*. Washington, D.C.: USDI Fish & Wildlife Service Special Science Report, Fish. No. 279.

NETTLESHIP, D. N., G. A. SANGER, AND P. F. SPRINGER. 1982. *Marine Birds: Their Feeding Ecology and Commercial Fisheries Relationships*. Compiled by the Canadian Wildlife Service for the Pacific Seabird Group. Ottawa, Ontario.

NORRIS, KENNETH S., ed. 1966. *Whales, Dolphins, and Porpoises*. Berkeley and Los Angeles: University of California Press.

ORNITHOLOGICAL SOCIETY OF JAPAN. 1974. *Check-list of Japanese Birds*. 5th ed. Tokyo: Gakken.

ORR, ROBERT T., AND ROGER C. HELM. 1989. *Marine Mammals of California*. Berkeley and Los Angeles: University of California Press.

PALMER, R. S., ed. 1962. *Handbook of North American Birds*. Vol. 1. New Haven: Yale University Press.

PENNY, M. 1974. *The Birds of the Seychelles and the Outlying Islands*. London: Collins.

PERRIN, W. F. 1975. Variation of Spotted and Spinner Porpoise (genus *Stenella*) in the Eastern Tropical Pacific and Hawaii. *Bulletin of the Scripps Institution of Oceanography* 21.

PETERSON, R. T. 1990. *A Field Guide to Western Birds*. 3d ed. Boston: Houghton Mifflin.

PITMAN, R. 1986. *Atlas of Seabird Distribution and Relative Abundance in the Eastern Tropical Pacific*. La Jolla, Calif.: U.S. National Marine Fisheries Service, Southwest Fisheries Center, Admin. Rep. LJ-86-02C.

PITMAN, R., AND S. M. SPEICH. 1976. Black Storm-petrel breeds in the United States. *Western Birds* 7(2): 71.

RICE, D. W., AND K. W. KENYON. 1962. Breeding distribution,

history, and populations of North Pacific Albatrosses. *Auk* 79:365–386.

RIDGELY, R. 1976. *A Guide to the Birds of Panama*. Princeton, N.J.: Princeton University Press.

ROBBINS, C. S., B. BRUUN, AND H. S. ZIM. 1983. *Birds of North America: A Guide to Field Identification*. Rev. ed. New York: Western Publishing Co., Golden Press.

ROBERSON, D. 1980. *Rare Birds of the West Coast 1980*. Pacific Grove, Calif.: Woodcock Publications.

SANGER, G. A. 1974. Pelagic studies of seabirds in the Central and Eastern Pacific Ocean. *Contrib. Zool.* 158:129–153.

SCRIPPS INSTITUTION OF OCEANOGRAPHY. 1987. *Surface Water Temperatures at Shore Stations, U.S. West Coast, 1986*. San Diego: University of California, Scripps Inst. of Oceanography, s10 Ref. 87-11.

SHIRIHAI, H. 1987. Shearwaters and other tubenoses at Eilat. *Dutch Birding* 9:152–157.

SLATER, P. 1970. *A Field Guide to Australian Birds: Non-passerines*. Adelaide, Australia: Rigby, Ltd.

SOWLS, ARTHUR L., A. R. DEGANGE, AND G. S. LESTER. 1980. *Catalogue of California Seabird Colonies*. Washington, D.C.: Coastal Ecosystems Project, U. S. Fish and Wildlife Service, U.S. Department of the Interior.

STALLCUP, R. 1976. Pelagic birds of Monterey Bay, California. *Western Birds* 7:113–136. Revised 1981.

STALLCUP, R., J. MORLAN, AND D. ROBERSON. 1988. First record of the Wedge-tailed Shearwater in California. *Western Birds* 19:61–68.

STEBBINS, ROBERT C. 1985. *A Field Guide to Western Reptiles and Amphibians*. 2d ed. Boston: Houghton Mifflin.

TYLER, W. B., AND K. BURTON. 1986. A Cook's Petrel specimen from California. *Western Birds* 17, no. 2.

U.S. FISH AND WILDLIFE SERVICE. 1980. *Beached Marine Birds and Mammals of the North American Coast: A Manual for the Census and Identification*. Biological Surveys Program FWS/obs-80/03.

WAHL, TERRENCE R. 1978. Seabirds in the Northwestern Pacific Ocean and South Central Bering Sea in June, 1975. *Western Birds* 9, no. 2.

WATSON, L. 1985. *Whales of the World: A Complete Guide to the World's Living Whales, Dolphins and Porpoises*. London: Hutchinson.

WINNETT, KATHY A., K. S. MURRAY, AND J. C. WINGFIELD. 1979. Southern race of Xantus' Murrelet breeding on Santa Barbara Island, California. *Western Birds* 10:81–82.

Glossary

AURICULARS: feathers on the side of a bird's head, covering its ear openings

AXILLARIES: elongate feathers in the region of a bird's "armpits"; the innermost wing linings

CARPAL: on or of a bird's wrist, the bend in its wing

COSTAL: on turtles, the large plates on the sides of the carapace between the outermost (marginal) plates and the centermost (vertebral) ones

CRISSAL: on or of a bird's undertail coverts (crissum)

MALAR: on the cheek of a bird

MELON: on cetaceans, a rounded or blunt head or forehead

NUCHAL: on the back of the neck

SCAPULARS: the large feathers on a bird's shoulders

TARSUS: the shank of a bird's leg—actually the straight part of its foot, just above the toes

ULNAR: the area of the large, forward bone (the ulna) in a bird's wing

About the Author

Rich Stallcup, one of North America's premier field ornithologists, is widely accomplished in wildlife observation, conservation, and teaching. Early in his career, Rich was a key player in the discovery that vagrant birds regularly migrate in a corridor including Point Reyes and the Farallon Islands. He participated in the founding of Point Reyes Bird Observatory in 1965 and has since led countless birding trips, from the Aleutians to the Rio Grande. An avid student of ocean life since childhood, Rich is a West Coast authority on the birds and mammals of the nearshore Pacific. He currently resides near the Point Reyes Peninsula with his daughter, Willow.

(Rod Norden)

Index

Boldface type refers to the major species descriptions. All other numbers indicate illustrations.